EPHESIANS
R. Paul Caudill

BROADMAN PRESS
NASHVILLE, TENNESSEE

4213-75

ISBN: 0-8054-1375-8

Dewey Decimal Classification: 227.5

Subject heading: BIBLE. N. T. EPHESIANS

Library of Congress Catalog Card Number: 78-67291

Printed in the United States of America

FOREWORD

"The New Testament is the Greek New Testament." Former students of the late professor W. Hersey Davis will recognize these measured words as those of our esteemed teacher. Dr. Davis was by no means opposed to translations of the Greek New Testament into English or other languages, but his reminder was that constant appeal must be made to the Greek text. No translation is final. No translation fully captures the intention of the text it seeks to render. Existing translations must be checked by the Greek New Testament, and fresh translations are proper as they seek to harvest the fruits of continuing study and give new expression to its findings in the language of the day.

Dr. Paul Caudill stands in the tradition of his mentors A. T. Robertson and W. Hersey Davis, a continuing student of the Greek New Testament and also a pastor-preacher committed to the full hermeneutical task of both hearing the word of God and proclaiming it afresh. Dr. Caudill is at home in the Greek New Testament and in articulating its intention in English. With the credentials for teaching, his vocational direction proved to be that of a teaching-preaching pastor. Throughout his pastoral ministry he lived daily with his Greek New Testament; and his speech, whether in formal or informal expression, was always in a chastened diction marked by clarity and precision.

Knowledge of Greek and knowledge of English are prerequisite to the right to offer a translation of the Greek New Testament in English. Dr. Caudill has these credentials. But more is required. A feel for the intention of the New Testament in its Greek expression and a compulsion to proclaim it responsibly and forcefully must be there, too. By these tests and more, Dr. Caudill has earned the right to offer a fresh translation. The result is a significant addition to a growing number of highly serviceable translations of Ephesians in English. This one is especially suited to the needs of pastors. It offers not only a translation but also supplementary notes containing basic information and insights regarding the Greek text.

FRANK STAGG
Senior Professor of New Testament
Interpretation

Southern Baptist Theological Seminary
Louisville, Kentucky

CONTENTS

DEDICATION

In memory of
my beloved teachers
Dr. A. T. Robertson
and
Dr. William Hersey Davis
former senior professors of
New Testament Interpretation
Southern Baptist Theological Seminary
Louisville, Kentucky

INTRODUCTION

"Of making many books there is no end," said the writer of Ecclesiastes, "and much study is a weariness of the flesh" (12:12). Whether there has been an overabundance of translations of the New Testament during the past few decades is a question we shall not endeavor to answer. After all, who is qualified to say that there is a plethora of translations in a field that yields such rich dividends for so many readers?

The late Dr. A. T. Robertson, one of the most widely known Greek grammarians of this century, and whose "Big Grammar" is to be found in most of the responsible libraries of the world, spoke intimately with me on Saturday afternoon before he died on Monday. I happened to be his last student assistant in Greek at the Southern Baptist Theological Seminary; and I had gone by his office to receive instructions concerning his class in Senior Greek, for he was expecting to be away from the class a number of times during the fall semester. In the midst of our conversation, he held up the Greek New Testament and said casually, "Paul, this book will speak to you, if you will allow it to do so, in a way it has never spoken to anyone else on this earth." He then went on to say that the translation of the Scriptures should be the last thing a man attempts to do. He was at the moment engaged in the translation of Matthew. Unfortunately, however, he had waited too long; for his effort was cut short two days later by death, leaving the work unfinished.

Dr. Robertson's words on that memorable Saturday afternoon served to stir me with desire to begin, some day, the translation of at least a portion of the New Testament. This I began some fifteen years ago, as I set my hand to the translation of the book of Ephesians. Only now is the work completed.

The decision to translate the book of Ephesians first evolved out of the growing impression that no other book in the New Testament, or in the Bible, is more relevant to the contemporary church. Somehow I saw in the book, as I lived with the text from day to day, something of the full purpose of God as he projected it in the advent of Christ. The more I dwelt with the content of the book, the more I came to believe that within its pages is a message capable of revolutionizing the life-style of the Christian and the local church. No other book in the Bible sets forth this unifying principle of God in Christ Jesus in such simple, straightforward terms as does Ephesians in chapters 1-3. What is more, no other book in the Bible, it appears to me, delineates so carefully and in such fullness the new life-style of the believer.

The apostle Paul boldly declared that "if anyone is in Christ, he is a new creation; the old has passed away, behold the new has come." Then he added, "All this is from God, who through Christ reconciled us to himself and gave us that ministry of reconciliation" (2 Cor. 5:17-18, RSV).

Throughout my pastorate of thirty-one years at the First Baptist Church of Memphis, Tennessee, I found the premise of this book, with its brilliant cascades of thought, to be a chief instrument of employ in my efforts to awaken the people and to implement their minds, their lives, and their possessions in the great stewardship and missionary objectives of our Lord. The measure of unity that pervades that historic church today and the bold, forward thrust in missions that now engages the church bear witness to the fruitfulness of the effort and to God's blessing on it.

In the translation I have endeavored to provide a work with outline and footnotes that will enable both the casual and the careful student of the Scriptures to have a helpful workshop in the building of sermons, devotional messages, or any type of dissertation or dialogue relating to the book of Ephesians.

It was also my hope that the translation and the footnotes would be meaningful to the casual or the careful reader of the Scriptures—to all who might desire to grow in their understanding of the message of Ephesians and of the full and unclouded purposes of God in Christ Jesus.

In the translation I have endeavored to do the following:

1. Translate directly from the Greek without the aid of other English translations.

2. Adhere, as literally as possible, to the Greek texts of Eberhard Nestle and Westcott and Hort, though the Greek text of the United Bible Societies has been consulted.

3. Use contemporary words as far as possible.

4. Avoid personal theological bias, endeavoring always to let the original Greek text speak for itself. It is easy for a translator to inject his own theology or presuppositions into a given passage; and from this I have earnestly endeavored to abstain.

5. Furnish a workable outline that is true to the author's intent.

6. Provide a minicommentary that deals helpfully with words and phrases on each page in the form of footnotes.

The outline that I have incorporated in the text may be helpful to both the student and the casual reader in that it helps one know the relation of a given passage to the whole.

At every point, I have attempted to translate the original Greek as literally as possible, and without textual comment. Occasionally there is a word or more in parenthesis to help make the passage read more smoothly.

By the use of extensive footnotes on each page, it was felt that perhaps such would help to obviate (for many readers) the need of a wide use of commentaries in the exploration of the true meaning of the text; for the footnotes reflect, hopefully, fruitful gleanings, in condensed form, from a host of commentaries on the book.

The Epistle

In nature's world as one beholds the handiwork of God in things of his creation, there are times when one can only stand in awesome wonder; for who can describe the penetrating beauty of a sunrise, a sunset, or the winds that blow? So it is with the letter to the Ephesians.

Coleridge, the great poet and philosopher, regarded Ephesians as "the divinest composition of man," embracing "first those doctrines peculiar to Christianity, and, then, those precepts common with it in natural religion." William Barclay called Ephesians "the supreme letter," while others have referred to it as "the queen of the epistles."

It is not our purpose here to deal with the critical problems that scholars in general have raised concerning Ephesians. Our purpose is to endeavor to let the radiant light of the epistle itself shine in all of its brilliance as it relates to the whole duty of the followers of Christ in their relationship to Christ and his church. After all, when all the diatribe has ended, incident to the critical problems that scholars throughout the ages have related to Ephesians, the work still stands, clad in garments of even more beautiful array and with a meaning that cannot pass away for all Christians!

Unlike any other book of the Bible, Ephesians serves to gather together, in one full sweep, the wide range of holy concepts of truth and duty as they emerge from our Judeo-

Christian heritage; and as one dwells upon this moving panorama of thought, he becomes strangely aware of his ability to perceive these truths and also of his capacity to apply them in the everyday walk of life. The letter is both theological and devotional and may be unsurpassed in its far and lofty reach of New Testament thought.

The epistle to the Ephesians, which is regarded as the "most general of all the Pauline epistles," has but few references to the immediate occasion. Chapters 1-3 describe "a solemn contemplation of the lofty privilege into which God's eternal purpose has brought believers in Christ," which is quickly followed in chapters 4-6 with a heart-searching exhortation to believers to walk worthily of the high calling in Christ Jesus. To quote Dr. James Hardy Ropes, "Beneath the simple structure of the epistle and pervading the whole is a fully developed conception of Christ as central in the universe and in history. God's purpose from eternity was in the fullness of times to unite in Christ the Jews (to whom had been given the covenants of promise) and so to bring home human history to its goal, the one New Man, the measure of the stature of the fullness of Christ."[1]

Paul closed the first half of the epistle with a prayer for the readers to be strengthened both in character and in the understanding of their calling (3:14-19) and with words of praise to the glory of God (3:20-21).

The epistle seems not only to endeavor to formulate "a philosophy of religion, which is at the same time a philosophy of history," but also "to bring them under the dominion of a single ruling theme—the eternal purpose of God to unite all things in heaven and on earth in Christ; and so to demonstrate their significance, not only for the particular social situation which first called forth their expression, but for the life of the church in all ages."[2]

The Occasion of the Writing

It must have been near the close of his ministry, and obviously Paul was in prison at the time of the writing of Ephesians, for he called himself "the prisoner of Christ Jesus in behalf of you Gentiles" (3:1). And he admonished his friends as "the prisoner in the Lord," meaning, of course, one actually in bonds. In 6:20 he spoke of himself as "an ambassador in a chain."

A careful examination of Ephesians and Colossians shows a close resemblance, whether viewed from a literary or a theological standpoint. The central position of Christ in relation to the universe is advanced in both the epistles. There is a striking similarity in the code of morals exhibited in the two epistles. (See Eph. 5:22 to 6:9; Col. 3:18 to 4:1.) Furthermore, many of the characteristic phrases, and in some instances whole verses, are similar. (See Eph. 1:7 and Col. 1:14; Eph. 1:10 and Col. 1:20; Eph. 1:21 and Col. 1:16; Eph. 1:22-23 and Col. 1:18-19; Eph. 2:5 and Col. 2:13; Eph. 2:11 and Col. 2:11; Eph. 2:16 and Col. 1:20; Eph. 3:2-3; and Col. 1:25-26, to mention a few of the parallels.)

Apparently Tychicus, referred to by Paul in Colossians 4:7, was the bearer of both the epistles, for in Ephesians 6:21-22 he told the Ephesians that he was sending Tychicus, his faithful brother and faithful minister in the Lord "whom I have sent to you for this very thing . . . so you may know the things concerning us and may comfort your hearts."

The letter is relatively free from the heat of controversy, being cast more in the form of a devotional meditation. The sharp play and thrust of dialectic that characterizes the other epistles of Paul is not found here. Rather, the train of thought "is marshaled in long and involved sentences, with clause linked to clause and phrase to phrase, the whole constructed with deliberation and forethought."[3] There are, however, striking peculiarities of vocabulary as well as differences of style. There are some eighty-two words found nowhere else in the Pauline letters, and thirty-eight of these words are found nowhere else in the New Testament.

The Recipients of the Epistle

In the days of Paul, there was no writing paper such as we have today. Letters and other forms of writing then were usually written on rolls of a substance called papyrus made from the pith of a plant that grew along the waters of the Nile and especially in the marshy places. Such letters were frequently rolled together, tied with a thread, and sealed if the matter were important or of a private nature. There was no need for an address since the letter was dispatched by hand. It was not thought necessary, therefore, for the New Testament letters to have titles; and in some instances these titles may have been inserted after the letters were collected and gathered together for the churches to read.

The letter to the Ephesians seems to have a mood that embraces not merely the church at Ephesus but perhaps all the churches of Asia Minor. Certainly the Gentiles figure prominently as recipients, for Paul referred to them as "formerly Gentiles in the flesh, called foreskin by the so-called circumcision, handmade, in the flesh" (2:11). Paul also admonished the recipients of the letter who were "in the Lord, to walk no longer as also the Gentiles walk in the vanity of their mind" (4:17). This mere fact in itself would not indicate that the letter was not written to Ephesus; but it does suggest that the recipients of the letter may have included a much wider scope than that of the membership at Ephesus alone.

Any way the epistle is viewed, it is perhaps best understood as a letter, circular in nature, intended for all the churches, Ephesus certainly being one of the group. If Paul had intended the letter for the church at Ephesus alone, **13** surely there would have been at least a few references in the epistle to the members and their relationships in the church at Ephesus.

Paul spent a great deal of time in Ephesus, certainly as much as three years (Acts 18:9-10). There was evidently also a close bond between Paul and the elders in Ephesus, for we have the record of his farewell message to them in Acts 20:17-35 when he was leaving Miletus on his last journey. Had Paul addressed the letter merely to the Ephesians, therefore, one would have expected a letter that was less impersonal, and at least sprinkled with personal touches throughout. The letter, on the other hand, is without personal greeting and lacks intimate expressions of fellowship that one finds in other Pauline letters.

The letter also suggests that Paul and at least some of the recipients were not too well acquainted with each other, for he wrote, "Wherefore, I too, having heard of your faith in the Lord Jesus and of your love toward all the saints, cease not giving thanks for you, constantly making mention of you in my prayers" (1:15-16). Paul also said, "For this cause I, Paul, the prisoner of Christ Jesus in behalf of you Gentiles—if so be that you have heard of the stewardship of the grace of God given unto me for you, how that according to revelation was made known to me the mystery just as I previously wrote to you briefly" (3:1-3). There seems to be implied here some doubt as to how well the recipients were acquainted with Paul's motivation for his special task. All in all, had Paul's words been intended primarily for the Christians at Ephesus, he would likely have clothed his thought a bit differently. It would seem that his words might have reflected a closer personal relationship such as he must have had with the church at Ephesus in the light of the time he spent there.

While Ephesians is directed in a special way to Gentile

Christians at large, one must remember that Tychicus carried the letter to particular readers of whom Paul had more than a general knowledge of their circumstances (1:15), and certainly these readers are to be distinguished from the expression "all the saints" found in 3:18 and 6:18. It is perhaps better to think of the intended recipients as being members of all the churches of Asia.

As one carefully reads the entire epistle, perceives the language as it "pours out like a cascade and a torrent," full of impassioned words, and views it from afar, he comes to feel that the letter is little less than a giant cornucopia filled with Judeo-Christian thoughts, bright and shining as the sun, that flow out in every direction as a spiritual harvest of fruitful thought to all the followers of Christ Jesus of every race and every nation.

What if the style varies in Ephesians? What if one finds words not found in any other Pauline epistle or in all the New Testament? Is this not a great writer's privilege? Is it not true of Shakespeare? What comparison is there between the styles of *A Midsummer Night's Dream* and *The Taming of the Shrew?*

Moreover, Paul wrote all of his epistles under different circumstances. Often he wrote, as one would say, "on the run"; but not so Ephesians. Then he was in prison! Then he had time for reflection, to vary his style, to introduce new words. As another has said, here one finds "the language of lyrical prayer, not the language of argument, and controversy, and rebuke."[4] Truly, "Ephesians was written to express new ideas, in very different circumstances, and—as we shall see—for a very different purpose from any of the other letters."[5]

The Thrust of the Epistle

Every parable spoken by Jesus seems to have a central

thrust. There is one point in the parable that is primary—one premise that is ever to be kept in mind and never forgotten. Even so in Ephesians Paul summarized the thought of the entire book in the opening chapter, verses 9 and 10, saying, "having made known to us the mystery of his will, according to his good pleasure, which he set forth in him, unto administration during the fullness of the times, so that all things might be gathered together in Christ, the things in the heavens and the things on the earth; in him." As another has well said:

> The key thought of Ephesians is the gathering together of all things in Christ. Christ is the center in whom all things unite, and the bond who unites all things. In nature as it is without Christ there is nothing but disunity and disharmony. There is battle in nature; nature is "red in tooth and claw." Man's dominion has broken the social union which should exist between man and the beasts. Man is divided from man; class from class; nation from nation; ideology from ideology; Gentile from Jew. The world, as we see it without Christ, is a divided, disunited, fragmented world. What is true of the world of outer nature is true of human nature itself. In every man there is a tension; every man is a walking civil war; there is a constant battle between the higher and the lower side of man; man is always torn between the desire for good and the desire for evil; he hates his sins and loves his sins at one and the same time.[6]

This estrangement between man and God, this cosmic battle that rages constantly between the powers of evil and the powers of good, this conflict that is ever present between angelic powers and evil spirits—between God and demons—is merely the result of a world without Christ. In such a world there could only be disunity. But this is not in accord with the purpose of God, with God's plan for man. God purposes in Christ a harmonious unity that embraces the whole world of man, for Christ is the unifying force in whom all things cohere.

Christians, those who have put their trust in Christ, constitute the church, the true body of Christ; and they are the visible, fruitful issue of Christ's redemptive work. Furthermore, Paul declared that the secret of the ages now stands revealed to men—the secret being the fact that the eternal purpose of God in Christ Jesus embraces the Gentiles as well as the Jews . . . that the gospel of Christ is for all men of every race and nation.

Course of Thought in the Epistle

The epistle to the Ephesians falls logically into two main divisions: chapters 1-3 in which the main thrust of the epistle is set forth; and chapters 4-6 in which Christian believers are called to a new life-style in the world. Following the salutation, Paul in rapid succession set forth the foundation of the plan (1:3-14) and the character of the plan (1:15 to 3:21). Then he dealt at length with the development of the new life-style of the Christian (Eph. 4—6). In this discussion Paul made first a stirring call to unity (4:1-6), discussed at some length the diversity of gifts (4:7-16), and then made a passionate plea for the abandonment of the old life-style (4:17-24). After dealing with sins which tend to fragment a church (4:25 to 5:14), the apostle entreated believers "to walk carefully and avoid drunkenness" (5:15-21), stressed the unity of family life (5:22 to 6:9), called boldly for moral rearmament on the part of the Christian (6:10-20), and closed with the benediction (6:21-24).

Some think that Paul's concept of the unity of all things in Christ (God's plan for man) might have derived from his experience in the Roman empire. As a Roman citizen (a fact of which he seemed to be proud), he had journeyed far and

17

wide throughout the empire and had come to see how a new, secular unity had been brought about in his part of the world through Rome.

> Now, in the Roman Empire a new unity had come to the world. The *pax Romana*, the Roman peace, was a very real thing. Kingdoms and states and countries, which had battled and struggled and competed and warred with each other, were gathered into a new unity in the Empire which was Rome. The barriers were down; the divisions were bridged; the hostilities were ended; the tensions were relaxed; all were gathered into one in Rome.[7]

This concept may have helped Paul come to realize, afresh, the necessity for the centrality of Christ in the world—how all things must be "gathered together in him, if a disunited nature and world and humanity were ever to be gathered into a unity." Certainly as a prisoner in Rome, after looking out over the vast reaches of the empire, the right frame of reference had been set for the guidance of the Holy Spirit as Paul penned his message to the Ephesians.

Following the translation and footnotes I have added, at the request of the publisher, some brief Explanatory Notes which I hope may be helpful to those who use the translation.

May I here record my grateful thanks to Dr. Frank Stagg of the Southern Baptist Theological Seminary for his careful reading of the manuscript, for his valuable suggestions, and for his Foreword. I would also express my appreciation for the thoughtful reading of the manuscript by a fellow pastor, Dr. Stanley Hahn of Georgia, and for his helpful suggestions. Finally, I would thank my capable secretary, Mrs. Eugenia Price, for her careful typing of the manuscript; and lastly my beloved wife, Fern, for her tireless and invaluable assistance in proofreading the manuscript and for her helpful suggestions.

The labor incident to this translation has been a rewarding experience from beginning to end, but the reward will be far greater if the translation proves to be helpful to others.

R. Paul Caudill

"Ferndale"
Vilas, North Carolina

Notes

1. *Encyclopaedia Britannica* 8 (Chicago: Encyclopaedia Britannica, Inc., 1943), p. 640.
2. *The Interpreter's Bible* 10 (Nashville: Abingdon Press, 1953), p. 604.
3. Ibid., p. 598.
4. William Barclay, *The Letters to the Galatians and Ephesians* (Philadelphia: The Westminster Press, 1958), p. 76.
5. Ibid.
6. Ibid., p. 77.
7. Ibid., p. 78.

Sources Mentioned in Notes on Translation

Robertson—*Word Pictures in the New Testament* 4 (Nashville: Broadman Press, 1931), *in loco.*

Souter — *A Pocket Lexicon of the Greek New Testament* (Oxford: Clarendon Press, 1916).

Stagg — Personal correspondence with Frank Stagg.

EPHESIANS
God's Plan for Man

CHAPTER 1

Salutation (1:1-2)

1   Paul, an apostle[1] of Jesus Christ because of[2] the will of God to those who are saints[3] (in Ephesus) and who are faithful[4] in Christ Jesus,

2   grace[5] to you and peace[6] from God our Father and our Lord Jesus Christ.

---

1. **apostolos**—One commissioned and sent forth by another to represent him in some way—an envoy, a delegate, messenger, missionary.

2. **dia**—On account of, by reason of, because of, for the sake of.

3. **hagiois**—Holy, sacred, consecrated; worthy of veneration; used of sacrifices and offerings prepared for God with solemn rites; in a moral sense, pure, sinless, upright; in the New Testament used of those whose lives are set apart for or unto God, to be exclusively his; hence saints.

4. **pistois**—Those who believe in Christ, who actively place their trust in him and rely (lean) upon him (with the entire human personality) for forgiveness, salvation, wisdom, guidance, strength.

5. **charis**—A lovely, unmerited, God-given experience of his favoring presence felt in the life of man. One can have peace only after he has received grace.

6. **eirene**—Related to *shalom* and so used by the ancient Hebrew scholars. The word means "well-being under God's sovereign rule." That tranquil state of mind and heart that is independent of circumstance and that results from being in Christ and in doing God's will in all things. Note: One must first receive grace before he can obtain peace.

I. The Foundation of the Plan (1:3-14)
A. God and Sonship (1:3-6)
(Our Eternal Choice to Sonship)

3   Blessed[7] be the God and Father of our Lord Jesus
     Christ, the one who blessed us with every spiritual
     blessing in the heavenly sphere[8] in Christ,
4   even as he chose[9] us in him before the foundation[10]
     of the world, to the end that we might be holy[11] and
     without blemish in his sight,[12] in love,
5   having designated[13] us beforehand for sonship
     through Jesus Christ unto himself,
6   according to the good pleasure of his will, unto praise
     of the glory of his grace, which he graciously be-

---

7. **eulogetos**—Used only of God and meaning "entitled to receive blessings from man."
8. **en tois epouraniois**—In the realm of spiritual activities—
   spiritual experience. The true abode of the citizen of Christ's
   kingdom is heaven. The contrast here is between the earthly
   and the heavenly sphere.
9. **exelexato**—Picked us out for himself. "The initiative is always
   with God—in creation, revelation, salvation. Election is not
   coercive, for we may freely respond; but if God did not choose
   us we could not choose him" (Frank Stagg).
10. **kataboles**—The depositing of the world, literally "the flinging
    or casting down" of the world.
11. Saints (see 1:1, footnote 3).
12. **katenopion**—Before the face of, before the presence of; that
    is, in the light of God's standard. While salvation is the free gift
    of God, on his own initiative, just as in creation and revelation,
    he in turn, receiving us as we are, calls us unto spiritual
    maturity-perfection (Matt. 5:48).
13. **proorisas**—To foreordain or "limit beforehand," literally
    "horizoned us off beforehand."

22

stowed[14] upon us in the beloved.[15]

B. Christ and Salvation (1:7-12)
(The Historical Redemptive Work of Christ)

7   In whom we keep on getting redemption[16] through his blood[17] the forgiveness[18] of our sins,[19] according to the riches of his grace,

8   which he caused to abound unto us in all wisdom[20]

---

14. *echaritosen*—From old word *charis,* grace (see 1:2, footnote 5).

15. *Egapemeno*—Perfect passive participle of *agapao,* meaning "I love." In the New Testament, never of the love between the sexes "but nearly always of the love of (the) God or (the) Christ to us, and of our love to him and to our fellow creatures, as inspired by his love for us" (Souter). One finds this phrase (referring to Jesus) nowhere else in the New Testament.

16. *apolutrosin*—Ransom, liberation, deliverance, emancipation—as of the setting free of a slave by his master.

17. *dia tou haimatos autou*—(cf. Col. 1:20). The blood of Christ is referred to here as ransom used in the liberation of slaves to effect their deliverance. Here it refers to the "cost" of our salvation. There is no reference as to a price paid to anyone (*lutron,* Matt. 20:28).

18. *aphesin*—A release, a letting go, a sending away, forgiveness, remission (in old inscriptions for remission from debt or punishment). The release from our sins. The costly key to the sinner's liberation.

19. *paraptomaton*—Originally, a fall beside or near something. A false step, a slip or trespass, a falling, a deviation from the truth and uprightness; a misdeed, a sin. Our sins—not Adam's (cf. Matt. 1:21).

20. *sophia*—Practical wisdom, heavenly and earthly; wisdom that has to do with "the eternal problems of life and death, and God and man, and time and eternity" (William Barclay).

and understanding[21]

9 having made known to us the mystery[22] of his will, according to his good pleasure, which he set forth in him,

10 for administration[23] during the fullness of the times, so that all things might be gathered together in Christ, the things in the heavens and the things on the earth;

11 in him, in whom we were also made an heritage, having been appointed beforehand according to the purpose[24] of him who works all things according to the counsel of his will,

12 so that we might be unto the praise of his glory—we who had put our hope beforehand in Christ;

C. The Holy Spirit and Promise (1:13-14)
(The Guaranteed Relationship of Believers)

13 in whom you also, having heard the word of the truth,

---

21. *phronesei*—Understanding that enables one to make choices which lead to right action in God's sight. Knowledge that enables one "to handle and to solve the day-to-day problems of practical life and living" (Ibid).

22. *musterion*—Something hidden, a secret, a mystery, not obvious to the understanding—a hidden purpose or counsel. Here the mystery refers to the fact that the Gentiles as well as the Jews are included in the scope of God's redemptive purpose in Christ Jesus. Previously this fact was not known to man.

23. *oikonomian*—An old word meaning household management, stewardship, the office of a steward—hence provision, arrangement, administration. The UBS (United Bible Societies) version has "which he will complete when the time is right."

24. *boulen*—Deliberate purpose, scheme, or plan.

24

the gospel of your salvation,[25] in whom also having believed (trusted) you were sealed[26] with the Holy Spirit of the promise,[27]

14 who is a pledge[28] (surety) of our inheritance unto the ransoming of his (God's) possession unto the praise of his glory.

II. The Character of the Plan (1:15 to 3:21)
A. Paul's Prayer for Growth in Understanding (1:15-19a)
1. The Occasion of the Prayer (1:15-16)

15 For this cause, I too having heard of your faith[29] in the

---

25. *soterias*—An old word (from *soter,* Savior) referring in extra-biblical language to bodily health, welfare, as of recovery from an illness—but also to victory over enemies and deliverance from every sort of calamity. In Christian terminology, the word refers to recovery of health from the disease of sin, including release from captivity to it, and salvation made possible by Jesus, the Messiah.

26. *esphragisthete*—To set a seal upon, to make with a seal, to place beyond doubt, to authenticate.

27. See John 14:25-26; 16:7,13-15; Acts 1:8; Luke 24:49.

28. *arrabon*—The Greek word *arrabon* (translated "earnest," "guarantee") was "a part of the purchase price of anything paid in advance and served as a guarantee and surety that the rest of the price, in due time, would be paid." The Holy Spirit was the down payment (but not the same idea of down payment as used today, for our down payments may be legally forfeited) or pledge of the incorruptible inheritance of all of heaven's joys in the last day. "God's gift of the Holy Spirit is the pledge, and first payment for the final inheritance in Christ" (A. T. Robertson).

29. *pistin*—Belief, trust; the leaning of the entire self upon God or Messiah in absolute trust and confidence for his salvation, wisdom, guidance, strength.

Lord Jesus and of your love toward all the saints,[30] do not cease giving thanks for you,

16 constantly making mention of you in my prayers,

2. General Nature of the Growth (1:17-18a)

17 that the God of our Lord Jesus Christ, the Father of glory, may give you the spirit of wisdom[31] and revelation with complete knowledge[32] of him,

18 having the eyes of your heart enlightened,

3. Special Objects of Knowledge (1:18b-19a)
   a. The Hope of His Calling (1:18b)
   b. The Glory of His Inheritance Among the Saints (1:18c)
   c. The Surpassing Greatness of His Power (1:19a)

so that you may know what is the hope of his calling,[33] what is the riches[34] of the glory of his inheritance among the saints,[35]

19 and what is the surpassing greatness of his power toward those of us who continually put our trust in him,

---

30. See 1:1, footnote 3.
31. See 1:8.
32. *epignosei*—Perception, discernment, recognition, experiential knowledge—that is precise and correct. In the New Testament, this word is used for knowledge of things ethical and divine.
33. *kleseos*—A call, an invitation; throughout the New Testament, used with reference to divine invitation to the individual "to embrace salvation in the kingdom of God." All the members of the body (the church) are regarded as being in a called relationship.
34. *ploutos*—Riches, wealth (material or spiritual).
35. See footnotes 3 and 30. Our riches are in God; God's riches are in his saints (A. T. Robertson).

B. The Grounds for the Plan (1:19b to 2:22)
1. The Exaltation of Christ (1:19b-23)

according to the working[36] of the gripping strength of his mighty power,[37]

20 which he put forth in Jesus Christ when he raised him from among the dead and seated him on his right hand in the heavens,

21 far above all rule and authority, and power, and lordship, and every name named[38] not only in this age but also in the coming age;

22 and put all things into subjection under his feet, and gave him[39] as head[40] over all things to the church,[41]

23 which is his body,[42] the fullness of him[43] who gives completeness to all things in every respect.

---

36. **energeian**—Working, active energy that is productive. In the New Testament, the word refers to "superhuman activity."

37. **ischuos**—Might, strength, force.

38. **pantos onomotos**—Here Paul listed some of the titles used by the pagans (Gnostics) in their speculations and declared the primacy for Jesus Christ above them all.

39. **edoken**—Gave him; put or placed him.

40. **kephalen**—Head, ruler, Lord. Christ is here declared to be the head of the church.

41. **ekklesia**—Literally, a calling out; then an assembly, a meeting, community congregation, society, church. Here, the body of believers of all time. "The term implies God's initiative and also his lordship. The English word 'church' is of another derivation (*kuriakos*—belonging to the Lord) but happily preserves a part of the implication of *ekklesia*" (Frank Stagg).

42. **autou**—That is, Christ's.

43. **tou pleroumenou**—"That filleth all in all." That is, Christ is the one who does the "filling." "The syntax permits either of two ideas: our fulfillment in Christ and his fulfillment in the church" (Ibid).

CHAPTER 2

2. The Mutual (Jew and Gentile) Past Experiences of God's Grace (2:1-10)

1
2
And you being dead in your trespasses[1] and sins[2] in which you formerly lived[3] according to the contemporary life-style of this world, according to the ruler of the authority of the air,[4] of the spirit of him who is now working in the sons of disobedience;[5]

3
among whom we[6] likewise all formerly lived in the desires of our flesh, doing the will of the flesh and of the minds, and we were by nature children of wrath[7]

---

1. *paraptomasin*—See 1:7.

2. *hamartiais*—A failing to hit the mark as with an arrow; an offense, evil deed, a violation of divine law in thought or act, sin.

3. *periepatesate*—Literally, walked around; in an ethical sense (Hebraistically), to live or conduct one's life.

4. *ton archonta tes exousias tou aeros*—Satan is pictured here as being ruler of the demons and evil agencies with whom man has to contend (A. T. Robertson). Jesus called Satan "the prince of this world" (John 16:11).

5. *huiois tes apeitheias*—Unbelievers in general; a Hebrew idiom like "sons of light" (see 1 Thess. 5:5). A reference to the power of Satan now at work in the lives of men.

6. *kai hemeis*—The Jewish converts.

7. *orges*—The principle of divine retribution whereby each sin carries with it its own condemnation. The punishment begins with the deed and is consummated at the judgment day—unless there is redemption.

like all the rest;[8]

4 but God being rich in mercy[9] because of his great love[10] with which he loved us,

5 even when we were dead in our trespasses, he made us alive together[11] with the Christ—by grace you have been saved—[12]

6 and he raised us up with him and caused us to sit together with him in the heavenly places[13] in Christ Jesus,

7 so that he might show forth[14] in the ages that are coming the surpassing[15] riches of his grace in kindness[16] toward us in Christ Jesus.

8 For by the grace you have been saved through faith;[17]

---

8. *hoi loipoi*—The Gentiles. Paul said that both Jews and Gentiles are subject to God's wrath on account of their sins.

9. *eleei*—The disposition and readiness to help those in trouble.

10. *agapen*—Affection, goodwill, "unconquerable benevolence"—love; the love of God toward men, of men toward God, and of men toward each other in Christ—the highest form of love.

11. *sunezoopoiesen*—To make one alive together with another. The reference is to the new moral and spiritual life in Christ (2 Cor. 5:17) and has to do with the spiritual resurrection of the believer who, without Christ, is "dead" in trespasses. As to Jesus, the resurrection was literal—he arose from the grave!

12. *sesosmenoi*—Perfect passive periphrastic indicative. The saving action of God took place in the past and still holds.

13. See 1:3.

14. *endeixetai*—To point out, demonstrate, manifest.

15. *huperballon*—From two Greek words, *huper* (over, beyond) and *ballo* (to cast, throw); hence to "exceed," "surpass."

16. *chrestoteti*—From *chrestois* (good; hence kindly, comfortable, not pressing); "kindliness," "kindness."

17. *dia pisteos*—Faith is the channel for the operation of the saving grace of God.

29

9　and that not out of you:[18] it is the gift[19] of God; not of works, so that no one may boast.[20]

10　For we are his workmanship[21] created in Christ Jesus for good works, which God prepared beforehand so that we might conduct[22] our lives accordingly (in them).

3. The Unification of Jew and Gentile in Christ (2:11-22)
a. The Former State of the Gentiles (2:11-12)

11　Therefore, remember forever that you were formerly Gentiles in the flesh, called foreskin by the so-called circumcision, handmade,[23] in the flesh[24]

12　that you were at that time without Christ, being alienated from the commonwealth[25] of Israel and strangers of the covenants[26] of the promise, having no hope

---

18. The source of salvation is "not in men, but from God" (A. T. Robertson).

19. *doron*—A gift, present from God; not something to be acquired by one's personal effort.

20. *kauchesetai*—To boast, glory in, exult proudly. In such glorying, the eyes are ever on self.

21. *poiema*—(From *poieo,* which means to "make," "construct," etc.) Creation, handiwork, workmanship; in the plural for "pieces of work."

22. *peripatesomen*—Literally to walk around "in them"—i.e., the good works; hence to conduct one's life, live.

23. *cheiropoietou*—Made or done by hand—hence, artificial.

24. *en sarki*—Hence, superficial.

25. *tes politeias*—Polity, citizen body, commonwealth; among the Romans the word signified "citizenship" or "citizen rights."

26. *ton diathekon*—The covenants with Abraham, Isaac, Jacob, David, etc.

and being without God[27] in the world.

b. New Relationship in Christ (2:13-18)

13 But now in Christ Jesus[28] you who were formerly far away have become near[29] by means of the blood[30] of Christ.

14 For he is our peace,[31] he who made both one, and broke down the middle wall[32] of partition,[33]

15 by having abolished, by means of his flesh, the enmity, the law of the commandments in decrees, so that he might create the two, in himself, into one new man,[34] making peace,

---

27. *atheoi*—Atheists in that they were without God and did not worship him.

28. *en Christo*—Note the frequent recurrence of this phrase in the epistle. The phrase is used to indicate the viable relationship that exists between the believer and Christ—those who have been "born of the spirit," "born again" (John 3:1-8). The expression may also refer, collectively, to his people, the church, the body of Christ.

29. *eggus*—"Near to the commonwealth of Israel in Christ."

30. *haimati tou Christou*—The pagans (Gnostics) denied the real humanity of Jesus. Here Paul declared the reality of Jesus' humanity in his role of Savior, Redeemer, and cleanser from sin.

31. *eirene*—See 1:2.

32. *mesotoichon*—The wall of separation between the Jews and the Gentiles. Paul doubtless had in mind the literal wall in the temple that separated the court of the Jews from that of the Gentiles. He may also have been looking back to his own eviction from the temple (Acts 21:28 ff.). Christ not only "broke down" this middle wall but also "split" the veil of the temple, thus giving all the saved an entrance to the holy place.

33. *phragmou*—Old word for "fence."

34. *kainon*—New in character, fresh, new; the spiritual, regenerated man (2 Cor. 5:17).

16   and reconcile[35] both in one body to God by way of the cross,[36] having slain the enmity by himself;

17   and having come, he preached peace to you who were far away,[37] and peace to those who were near,[38]

18   for through him we both have access[39] by one Spirit[40] to the Father.

c. The New Citizenship Restated (2:19-22)

19   Therefore you are no longer strangers and sojourners, [41] but rather you are fellow citizens[42] of the saints and the household of God,

20   having been built upon the foundation of the apostles

---

35. **apokatallaxe**—Old word from *apo,* "from," and *katallasso,* to "change," "exchange" (as of coins); hence to reconcile, restore completely; to bring back to a former state of harmony—one that is completely "other." One of Paul's great doctrinal words. God in his great love for all is engaged in reconciling us to himself by means of (*dia*) his son, who serves as the Lamb of Sacrifice.

36. **dia tou staurou**—Literally through the cross, by means of the cross. On the cross Christ "slew" the enmity that existed between Jew and Gentile.

37. **tois makran**—Those with no hope in God—Gentiles.

38. **tois eggus**—The Jews.

39. **prosagogen**—Entrée, access, approach, "beachhead"—as for a landing.

40. **Pneumati**—The Holy Spirit.

41. **xenoi kai paroikoi**—A resident without city rights—a foreigner, originally; one belonging to another country or to another community within the same country; one who is merely a "sojourner" in a land other than his own. A noncitizen with limited rights.

42. **sunpolitai**—Possessing the same citizenship as all who are of the household of God (see 2:12).

and prophets, Christ Jesus himself being the chief cornerstone,[43]

21 in whom every building properly fit together[44] will grow into a sanctuary[45] holy in the Lord,

22 in whom also you are being built together for a dwelling place[46] of God in the Spirit.

---

43. *akrogoniaiou*—"The primary foundation stone at the angle of the structure by which the architect fixes a standard for the bearings of the work and crosswalls throughout" (W. W. Lloyd).

44. *sunarmologoumene*—A lovely architectural metaphor (see 1 Pet. 2:5).

45. *naon hagion*—Used of the temple shrine—the part of the temple where God himself dwelt.

46. *katoiketerion*—Habitation. In 1 Corinthians 3:16 Paul called each believer a *naos Theou* (temple of God) in which the Spirit of God dwells.

CHAPTER 3

C. Paul's Own Mission in the Plan (3:1-9)

1 For this cause[1] I, Paul, the prisoner[2] of Christ Jesus in behalf of you Gentiles—

2 if so be that you have heard[3] of the stewardship of the grace of God given unto me for you,

3 how that according to revelation[4] was made known to me the mystery,[5] just as I previously wrote[6] to you briefly,[7]

4 so that you might be able by reading to realize my understanding in the mystery of Christ,

5 which in other generations was not made known to the sons of men as now has been revealed to his holy apostles and prophets in the Spirit,

---

1. *toutou charin*—Referring to his preceding words concerning God's elective grace.
2. *ho desmios*—One bound in chains—a captive. Paul, in prison at Rome, was chained to the wrist of a Roman soldier and awaiting trial before Nero.
3. Note: 3:2-13 forms a long parenthesis. The train of Paul's thought jumps the track; but it comes back on the track at verse 14.
4. *apokalupsin*—An uncovering, unveiling, a revealing.
5. See 1:9.
6. *proegrapsa*—To write previously (aforetime); evidently a reference to a "lost" letter as in 1 Corinthians 5:9.
7. *en oligo*—In a few words.

34

6 how that the Gentiles are fellow-heirs and fellow-members of the same body[8] and fellow-sharers of the promise in Christ Jesus through the gospel,

7 of which I became a minister[9] according to the free gift of the grace of God given to me according to the working of his power.

8 To me, the more least[10] of all saints, was this divine favor[11] given to proclaim to the Gentiles the good news concerning the incomprehensible[12] riches of Christ,

9 and to bring to light the character of the stewardship of the mystery[13] hidden from of old in God who created all things,

D. The Mission of the Church (3:10-13)

10 so that now might be made known to the principalities and to the powers[14] in the heavenly sphere,

---

8. **sunsoma**—From *sun,* "together," and *soma,* "body"; hence belonging to the same body (by metaphor "the same church"). The church (called-out body of believers) is the body of Christ.

9. **diakonos**—A servant, ministering attendant; one who executes the commands of another. Hence our word "deacon." The term as Paul used it was "still fluid, not yet technical."

10. **elachistotero**—Here a comparative form (*teros*) of an adjective is added to the superlative form of an adjective (*elachistos*), which means "least," "smallest," "very little." Hence "the more least."

11. **charis**—See 1:2.

12. **anexichniaston**—That cannot be tracked out; unsearchable, inexplorable.

13. See 1:9; 3:3.

14. **exousiais**—Leading men, leaders, governors, earthly powers.

through the church,[15] the much-varied[16] wisdom of God,

11   according to the eternal purpose[17] which he projected[18] in Christ Jesus our Lord,

12   in whom we have freedom of speech and access[19] in confidence through faith in him.[20]

13   Therefore I beg you not to lose heart[21] in thinking about my trials[22] in your behalf, which are your glory.[23]

E. Paul's Prayer for His Readers (3:14-21)

14   For this cause[24] I bow my knees to the Father,

15   from whom every family[25] in heaven and on earth gets its name,

---

15. *ekklesias*—The body of Christ set forth in chapter 2 (see 1:22).

16. *polupoikilos*—Manifold, variegated, of variety of colors, much varied, very varied.

17. *prothesin*—Deliberate purpose, scheme, plan.

18. *epoiesen*—To do, make, construct, fashion, produce, provide, achieve.

19. *prosagogen*—An entrée, a landing stage, beachhead.

20. *autou*—That is, Christ.

21. *enkakein*—A rare and late word from *en* and *kakos* and meaning "to behave badly in, to give in to evil (in a cowardly manner)."

22. *thlipsesin*—From *thlibo,* to press hard upon—as grapes in the winepress. Persecution, distress, affliction.

23. *doxa*—"An especially divine quality, the unspoken manifestation of God," the Shekinah (in Jewish theology, the divine presence); honor, praise, glory, splendor, excellence, etc.

24. *toutou charin*—For this cause; here the long parenthesis ends and Paul picked up where he left off in verse 2.

25. *patria*—In Old Testament days a word commonly used of a group of persons united by descent from a common ancestor or father. Hence a tribe, a family.

16 that he may endow[26] you with power[27] according to the riches of his glory to be strengthened through his Spirit in the inner man,[28]

17 to the end that Christ, through faith,[29] may permanently dwell[30] in your hearts, being thoroughly rooted[31] and established[32] in love,[33]

18 so that you may have the strength to comprehend[34] with all the saints what is the breadth and the length and the height and the depth,

19 and come to know[35] by your own experience the love of Christ which surpasses[36] this knowledge, so that

---

26. **do**—From *didomi.* To give, offer, grant, endow.

27. **dunamei**—(Physical) power, force, might. (Our English word "dynamite" comes from this word.)

28. **ton eso (anthropon)**—The inside (within) man as opposed to the outward (*exo*) man. The Greeks associated reason, conscience, and will with the "inner man."

29. **dia tes pisteos**—Faith is the channel through which the indwelling Christ is experienced.

30. **katoikesai**—To dwell, to settle in, to be established in (with idea of permanency), "to make one's home, to be at home."

31. **errizomenoi**—To root, strengthen with roots, render firm, fix, establish a person or thing.

32. **tethemeliomenoi**—To found, lay a foundation, establish, make stable.

33. **en agape**—These words "in (or with) love" might go with the participles "rooted and established" or with *katoikesai,* "to dwell."

34. **katalabesthai**—Seize tight hold of, arrest, capture, appropriate, comprehend, perceive.

35. **gnonai**—To take in knowledge, learn, come to know, understand, perceive—a knowledge based on personal experience.

36. **huperballousan**—To exceed, excel—as to throw over or beyond anything; to surpass, transcend.

you may be filled with respect to all the fullness of God.

20 And to the One who is able, beyond everything, to do superabundantly[37] more than we ask for ourselves or think, accordingly to the power[38] that is working[39] in us,

21 to him be the glory[40] in the church and in Christ Jesus unto all the generations of all the ages; amen.

---

37. *huperekperissou*—Beyond measure; most exceedingly.
38. *dunamin*—God's power (see 3:16).
39. *energoumenen*—That is energizing in us, being made to work in us.
40. See 3:13.

CHAPTER 4

III. The Development of the New Life-Style of the Christian (4—6)
A. A Stirring Call to Unity (4:1-6)

1   I entreat you therefore, I the prisoner[1] in the Lord, to walk worthily[2] of the calling wherewith you were called,

2   with all humility[3] and meekness,[4] with longsuffering, supporting[5] one another with love,

3   seriously striving[6] to keep the unity of the Spirit with the bond of the peace;

4   one body[7] and one Spirit,[8] even as you were called in

---

1. *ho desmios*—As in 3:1.

2. *axios*—In a manner worthy of, worthily, suitably.

3. *tapeinophrosunes*—Modesty, lowliness of mind, self-knowledge that comes from self-evaluation based on the life-style of Christ and the commands of God.

4. *prautetos*—From an old word *praus* meaning mild, meek, gentle, and used by the Greek for an animal completely domesticated, trained, and under control. Hence, in Christian terminology, a meek man is one whose life is completely subject to the disciplines of Christ and God the Father.

5. *anechomenoi*—To hold up, bear with, endure, sustain, support.

6. *spoudazontes*—To be zealous, be eager, hasten.

7. *soma*—The mystical body of Christ, the born-again believers of all time—"the spiritual church."

8. *Pneuma*—One Holy Spirit.

one hope[9] of your calling;

5 one Lord,[10] one faith,[11] one baptism;[12]

6 one God[13] and Father of all, the One who is over[14] all and through[14] all and in[14] all.

B. Diversity of Gifts (4:7-16)

7 And to each one of us the grace was given according to the measure of the free gift of Christ.

8 Wherefore he says, Having ascended[15] on high he took captivity captive;[16] he gave gifts[17] to men.

9 And what is the ascension except that he descended into the lower part of the earth;

---

9. *elpidi*—The same hope for both Jew and Greek—that all men might come to know redemption in Christ as Savior and Lord. "This is not the hope which springs from the human heart. It is the hope which God places before us. The hopes of mankind often fail. God offers a hope which is certain" (Frank Stagg).

10. *Kurios*—This word may well refer to Jesus in view of Paul's frequent use of the word in this context and of other apostles' use of it (see John 20:25). Certainly the usage could mean Jesus as well as God (cf. John 10:30).

11. *pistis*—See 2:15. One saving trust—with Christ as its object.

12. *baptisma*—A dipping, immersion, submersion; a public act of commitment to Christ and testifying to the believer's faith in the resurrection of Christ and in his own resurrection to a new life now and in the final resurrection of the dead.

13. *eis Theos*—One God—not a tribal god or "separate God for each nation or religion" (A. T. Robertson).

14. *epi ... dia ... en*—Prepositions reflecting the power (control), providence, and presence of God (William Barclay).

15. *anabas*—To go up, mount, ascend.

16. *aichmalosian*—As in war.

17. *domata*—Pagan emperors demanded gifts from those whom they conquered. Christ gave gifts to those he conquered.

10 and the one who came down[18] is the same one who ascended[19] above all the heavens, in order that he might give fullness to all things.

11 And he, he gave some to be apostles,[20] and some prophets,[21] and some evangelists,[22] and some shepherds[23] and teachers,[23]

12 for the perfecting[24] of the saints unto a work of ministering,[25] unto the upbuilding of the body of Christ,

13 until we all attain unto the oneness of the faith and of the knowledge of the Son of God, unto a full-grown[26] man, unto the measure of the stature of the fullness of Christ,

---

18. *katabas*—The incarnation. Otherwise the reference would be to Christ's death and descent into hades (Acts 2:31).

19. *anabas*—The ascension, it would seem. Verse 10 apparently supports this view.

20. *apostolous*—As in 1:1.

21. *prophetas*—A man endowed to tell forth the will of God in speech whether of present or future.

22. *euaggelistas*—A missionary, bearer of the good news to man, an evangelist.

23. *poimenas*—A herdsman, shepherd; root meaning is "to protect" (see John 10:11; 1 Pet. 2:25). One who tends, feeds, protects the flock; hence, our word pastor (from Latin *pastores*). Note that shepherds and teachers (*didaskalous*) are grouped together. More than one gift may be given to the same man.

24. *katartismon*—To fit (join) together, mend, equip, repair, bring to proper condition.

25. *diakonias*—All the saints (the whole body of Christ) are to be ministering servants in whatever measure God equips them for service to the end that all of the body of Christ may be edified.

26. *teleion*—Mature, complete.

41

14 so that we are no longer children tossed about as in a storm at sea and swung around[27] by every wind of teaching in the trickery[28] of men, in cleverness on the side of error,

15 but speaking the truth in love let us grow into him[29] in all respects who is the head, Christ,

16 out of whom all the body, being fit together[30] and united[31] through the supply of every joint according to the working[32] in the measure of each measure, part by part, produces the growth of the body for the building up of itself in love.

C. A Plea for the Abandonment of the Old Life-Style (4:17-24)
1. The Old Life-Style (4:17-19)

17 This I therefore say and solemnly charge[33] you in the Lord, to walk no longer as also the Gentiles walk in the vanity[34] of their mind,

18 being darkened in the understanding,[35] being alien-

---

27. *peripheromenoi*—Old word to carry around, swing around, whirl around (as by wind).

28. *kubia*—Literally, playing with dice, gaming; hence "trickery."

29. *eis Auton*—That is, Christ (see metaphor in v. 13).

30. *sunarmologoumenon*—An architectural term where *harmos* means "the side of a stone." The larger word refers to "fitting together" the stone.

31. *sunbibazomenon*—To bring together, join, put together.

32. *energeian*—Working, action productive of work, activity.

33. *marturomai*—Summon or call to witness, testify.

34. *mataioteti*—Emptiness, purposelessness, ineffectiveness, vanity, unreality.

35. *dianoia*—From *dia, nous*. Probably including both the intellect and emotions (A. T. Robertson).

ated[36] from the life of God, because of the ignorance among them, because of the hardening[37] of their heart,

19 who, having ceased to care,[38] gave themselves over to shocking conduct,[39] in the practice of every uncleanness with greediness.[40]

2. The New Life-Style (4:20-24)

20 But you, you did not so learn[41] the Christ
21 if indeed you heard him and were taught by him, even as there is truth in Jesus,
22 to put off[42] the old man according to the former[43] life-style,[44] which is morally corrupting according to the lusts of deceit,

---

36. **apellotriomenoi**—To be alienated from; in this particular verb form the word is "practically a noun"—aliens.
37. **porosin**—Petrifaction, hardness, numbness, deadness, a callus; hence a dulling of the faculty of perception, intellectual (moral) blindness.
38. **apelgekotes**—Cease to feel pain, be past feeling; cease to care.
39. **aselgeia**—Conduct shocking to public decency, lewdness, wantonness.
40. **pleonexia**—Covetousness, always wanting more (whether of sexual indulgence, as here, or money) and with complete disregard of the rights of others, greediness.
41. **emathete**—Old word to learn, to increase one's knowledge.
42. **apothesthai**—The metaphor is that of putting off garments, clothing.
43. **proteran**—First of two, former, on a previous occasion, earlier, formerly.
44. **anastrophen**—Manner of life, life-style.

23 and to keep on being renewed[45] in the spirit of your mind,

24 and to put on the brand new man[46] that is created[47] according to God's pattern[48] in righteousness and holiness of the truth.

D. Teaching Against Sins That Tend to Fragment a Church (4:25 to 5:14)

25 Wherefore, having put away[49] the lying, keep on speaking truth, each one with his neighbor, for we are members[50] of one another.

26 Be ye angry and sin not;[51] let not the sun set on your wrath;[52]

27 neither give a place to the devil.

28 The one who has the habit of stealing is no longer to steal, but rather he is to labor, working with his own hands the good thing, so that he may have something to share[53] with the one who has need.

29 No corrupt (rotten) word is to proceed out of your mouth, but if something is good, it is to be for the

---

45. *ananeousthai*—Old verb "to make new (young) again"—only here in New Testament.
46. *kainon anthropon*—The new man, new manner of life, new life-style, new in essential quality, character.
47. *ktisthenta*—Old verb to create, make, found—always of God.
48. *kata Theon*—After God, according to God—the new life in Christ, new birth.
49. See 4:22.
50. *mele*—Bodily organ, limb, member.
51. See 2:1, footnote 2.
52. *parorgismo*—Indignation, exasperation, provocation, wrath.
53. *metadidonai*—To impart, share a thing with another.

upbuilding[54] of the need so that it may bestow a favor on those who hear.

30 And do not grieve the Holy Spirit of God, with whom you were sealed[55] unto the day of redemption.[56]

31 And every kind of bitterness, and anger, and wrath, and clamour,[57] and blasphemy[58] are to be removed from you together with all wickedness.

32 And keep on becoming kind toward one another, tenderhearted,[59] forgiving one another just as also God in Christ forgave you.

---

54. *oikodomen*—Edification, improvement, the act of building, building up; hence edification.
55. See 1:13.
56. *hemeran apolutroseos*—"The day when final redemption is realized" (A. T. Robertson).
57. *krauge*—A shout, clamor, cry, outcry (clamoring against one another).
58. *blasphemia*—Abusive or scurrilous language.
59. *eusplagchnoi*—Merciful, tenderhearted. Similar to the word used in Matthew 9:36 to describe the feeling Jesus had for the multitudes as he looked upon them in their distressful condition.

CHAPTER 5

1   Keep on becoming, therefore, imitators[1] of God, as children beloved;

2   and continue to make love your life-style,[2] even as the Christ also loved you and gave himself for us as an offering[3] and a sacrifice to God for an odor[4] of a sweet smell.[5]

3   But sex outside of marriage[6] and every impurity or covetousness,[7] is not even to be mentioned[8] among you, as is becoming to saints;[9]

4   and baseness[10] and foolish talking[11] or facetious

---

1. *mimetai*—To imitate, mimic, copy in action.

2. *peripateite en agape*—Keep on walking around in love, conduct oneself, regulate one's life.

3. *prosphoran*—A gift, present, an offering (especially to God) for sin.

4. *osmen*—Odor, smell; "originally of the sweet-smelling odor of sacrifice" (Souter).

5. *euodias*—A sweet smell.

6. *porneia*—Fornication, habitual immorality (the practice of consorting with prostitutes).

7. *pleonexia*—Covetousness, greediness, rapacity—with utter disregard of the rights of others.

8. *mede onomazestho*—Literally, name not, give not a name to. The ancient Greeks held that to talk about an evil and undesirable thing was to bring it a step nearer to favor and action.

9. *hagiois*—See 1:1, footnote 3.

10. *aischrotes*—Baseness, dishonor.

11. *morologia*—Not too far removed in meaning from what one might call "moron talk."

prattle,[12] which things are not becoming, but rather the giving of thanks.

5 For this ye know, recognizing by your own experience, that every male prostitute[13] or impure person or covetous person,[14] which is an idolator,[15] has no inheritance in the kingdom of Christ and God.

6 No one is to deceive you with empty[16] words; for because of these things the wrath[17] of God ever comes upon the sons of disobedience.[18]

7 Don't you become, therefore, their partners;[19]

8 for you were formerly darkness, but now you are light in the Lord; as children of light continue to conduct yourselves—[20]

9 for the fruit of the light *is* in all goodness and righteousness and truth—

10 testing[21] what is well-pleasing to the Lord;

11 and do not have fellowship with the unfruitful works

---

12. *eutrapelia*—Facetiousness, raillery, low jesting.

13. *pornos*—Literally, male prostitute, a man who indulges in sexual intercourse outside of marriage.

14. *pleonektes*—A person who is greedy, self-aggrandizing, covetous, a defrauder; one who tramples on the rights of others to attain his goal or satisfy his desires (see 4:19).

15. *eidololatres*—A worshiper of an image.

16. *kenois*—Vain, empty, foolish, worthless, ineffective, false, pretentious, hollow, unreal (see Col. 2:4 f.). Maybe a reference to the Gnostics.

17. See 2:7.

18. See 2:2.

19. *sunmetochoi*—Fellow-sharers.

20. *peripateite*—Literally, walk about, conduct one's life (see 2:10).

21. *dokimazontes*—To put to the test, examine, prove, think fit, approve after testing.

of the darkness, but rather also reprove[22] such;

12 for the things being done by them in secret it is shameful even to speak of;

13 for all the things that are reproved[23] by the light are plainly recognized;[24] for the thing that makes everything clear is light;

14 wherefore he says: Wake up,[25] you sleeper, and rise up[26] from among the dead, and Christ will shine upon you.

E. Exhortation to Walk Carefully and Avoid Drunkenness (5:15-21)

15 Be extremely careful[27] how you conduct yourself, not as unwise but as wise,

16 buying up for yourselves the opportunity,[28] because the days are evil.

17 Therefore, don't become foolish,[29] but understand[30]

---

22. *elegchete*—To expose, convict, reprove, "convict by turning the light on the darkness" (A. T. Robertson).

23. *elegchomena*—See 5:11.

24. *phaneroutai*—To make clear, visible, manifest.

25. *egeire*—To wake, arouse, raise up.

26. *anasta*—To raise up, set up, rise (especially) from among the dead—dead bodies. Possibly an adaptation or reference to Isaiah 26:19; 60:1.

27. *blepete*—Look, see . . . carefully, exactly, strictly.

28. *exagorazomenoi*—A sort of marketplace term meaning to buy out, ransom, purchase out, buy, redeem, buy away from (see Col. 4:5).

29. *aphrones*—Senseless, stupid, without reflection on intelligence, of one who acts rashly.

30. *suniete*—To put or bring together, to join together in the mind.

what the will of the Lord is.

18 And don't get drunk with wine, in which state there is no salvation,[31] but be constantly filled with the Spirit,

19 speaking to yourselves in psalms and hymns[32] and spiritual songs,[33] singing and playing on the harp in your heart to the Lord,[34]

20 giving thanks at all times in behalf of everything in the name of our Lord Jesus Christ to the God and Father,

21 subordinating[35] yourselves to one another in the fear of Christ.

F. The Unity of the Family Life (5:22 to 6:9)

22 The wives are to be to their own husbands as to the Lord,

23 for a husband is head[36] of the (his) wife as also the Christ is head of the church, he being the savior of the body.

24 Nevertheless, as the church is subject to the Christ, so also the wives are to be to their husbands in everything.

25 Husbands, keep on loving your wives even as the Christ also loved the church and gave himself for it,

---

31. *asotia*—Wantonness, profligacy, an abandoned, dissolute life in which condition there is no hope of deliverance (salvation).

32. *humnois*—A hymn, especially of praise to God.

33. *odais*—An ode, song, lay—used in the Scriptures of songs that praise God or Christ (Rev. 15:3).

34. *to Kurio*—The Lord Jesus—another accent on his deity.

35. *hupotassomenoi*—To put in a lower rank, to rank under (a military term), to subordinate self, submit self, put self in subjection.

36. *kephale*—Head, metaphor of anything supreme, chief, prominent (as of persons).

26 in order that he might sanctify[37] it, having cleansed it with the washing of the water,[38] in a word,

27 in order that he himself might present to himself the church glorious, not having a spot[39] or a wrinkle[40] or any such things, but that it might be holy[41] and without blemish.[42]

28 So ought also the men to love their own wives as their own bodies. The one who loves his own wife loves himself;

29 for no one ever hated his own flesh, but nourishes and cherishes it, just as also the Christ did the church,

30 for we are members of his body.[43]

31 For this cause a man shall leave his father and his mother and shall be joined to[44] his wife, and the two shall be unto one flesh.[45]

32 This mystery is great, but I, for my part, speak with reference to Christ and the church.

---

37. *hagiase*—To set apart to or for God, to treat as holy (set apart) (see 1:1, footnote 3).

38. *hudatos*—Some see here a reference by analogy to the bath of the bride before marriage as practiced among the ancient Jews.

39. *spilon*—Moral blemish, fault.

40. *hrutida*—A wrinkle of age.

41. *hagia*—See 1:1, footnote 3.

42. *amomos*—Without blemish, unblemished—as of sacrificial animals.

43. *somatos*—The human body—figuratively, of the church as his body.

44. *proskollethesetai*—Literally to glue one thing to another, join or unite closely, cleave to, stick to.

45. *eis sarka mian*—i.e., in the birth of their child.

33   Nevertheless, each one of you also is so to love his own wife as himself, and the wife is to treat her husband with deep respect.[46]

---

46.   *phobetai*—Here the meaning is to reverence, venerate, treat with deference, reverential obedience, to treat with deep respect.

CHAPTER 6

1   Children, obey your parents in the Lord; for this is right.[1]

2   Honor[2] your father and your mother, which is a foremost commandment with a promise:[3]

3   that it may be well with you and that you may be a long time on the earth.

4   And fathers, do not irritate[4] your children, but bring them up[5] in the discipline[6] and counsel of the Lord.

5   Slaves, be obedient to your human masters with fear and trembling in sincerity[7] of your heart as to the Christ,

6   not with eye-service[8] as men pleasers, but as slaves of Christ doing the will of God from the heart,[9]

7   with goodwill as slaving for the Lord and not for men,

---

1. *dikaion*—Just in the eyes of God, righteous; in Colossians 3:20 one finds *euareston* (well-pleasing).

2. *tima*—To revere, venerate, honor, give honor to.

3. See Exodus 20:12.

4. *parorgizete*—To rouse to wrath, provoke, exasperate, anger.

5. *ektrephete*—To nourish up to maturity, nurture, bring up.

6. *paideia*—The whole education and training of children—both with reference to mind and morals; education, training, discipline.

7. *haploteti*—Sincerity, singleness of mind.

8. *ophthalmodoulian*—Enslavement to the eye—"the subjection that waits upon a glance of a master's eye" (Souter).

9. *ek psuches*—The idea here approaches that of "self"; hence the psychic sense of "desire."

8   knowing that whatever good thing each shall have done, he will receive it back from the Lord, whether enslaved or free.

9   And masters, continue to do these same things to these, giving up the threatening,[10] knowing that both their Lord and yours is in the heavens, and there is no favoritism[11] with him.

G. The Christian Armor (6:10-20)

10   From now on, be strengthened[12] in the Lord and with the power of his might.

11   Put on[13] the complete armor[14] of God so you may be able to stand against the crafty methods[15] of the devil;

12   because for us the wrestling[16] is not against blood and flesh, but against the principalities, against the authorities, against the world tyrants of this darkness, against the spiritual elements of wickedness in the heavenly places.[17]

13   Therefore, take up the complete armor of God in

---

10. *apeilen*—Threatening, a threat.
11. *prosopolempsia*—Respect of persons, partiality, face-receiving.
12. *endunamousthe*—Passive form. To receive strength, be strengthened (here in union with the Lord).
13. *endusasthe*—Put on oneself, be clothed with.
14. *panoplian*—Full armor, complete armor, literally all the armor.
15. *methodias*—Scheming, craftiness, methods.
16. *pale*—A wrestling bout, struggle, conflict.
17. *epouraniois*—In the heavenly sphere, the sphere of spiritual activities. The evil foes are both natural and supernatural. Hence the need for the full armor of God.

order that you may be able to withstand[18] in the evil day, and having accomplished all still to stand[19] victoriously.

14 Take your stand therefore having girded your loins with truth, and having put on the breastplate of righteousness,

15 and having shod your feet with the readiness[20] of the gospel of peace;

16 in everything taking up the shield of the faith, with which you will be able to quench[21] all the fiery darts of the wicked one;

17 and receive[22] the helmet of salvation[23] and the sword of the Spirit, which is the word[24] of God,

18 through all prayer and supplication, praying on every occasion[25] in the Spirit, and watching thereto with all perseverance[26] and entreaty concerning all the saints;

19 and in behalf of me, that utterance may be given unto

---

18. *antistenai*—To take a stand against, resist, oppose.

19. *stenai*—After having gone through each stage of the conflict, still to stand victoriously!

20. *hetoimasia*—Readiness, that is, of mind. The gospel helps produce this.

21. *sbesai*—To extinguish, put out.

22. *dexasthe*—To receive, take up, embrace, make one's own.

23. *soteriou*—See 1:13.

24. *hrema*—A spoken word, an utterance, and consequently the gospel, Christian teaching, God's Word, which is "sharper than any two-edged sword" (Heb. 4:12).

25. *en panti kairo*—"On every occasion."

26. *proskarteresei*—To persevere, give constant attention to, continue steadfast.

me in the opening of my mouth, with boldness[27] to make known the mystery of the gospel,

20 in behalf of which I am an ambassador in a chain, that I may speak boldly therein as it is necessary for me to speak.

H. Benediction (6:21-24)

21 And in order that you also may know how things go with me, how I fare, Tychicus[28] my beloved brother and faithful servant in the Lord,

22 whom I sent to you for this very thing, will make everything known to you, so you may know the things concerning us and may comfort your hearts.

23 Peace to the brethren and love with faith from God the Father and the Lord Jesus Christ.

24 The grace be with all who continue to love our Lord Jesus Christ in purity.[29]

---

27. *parresia*—Boldness, freedom, liberty in speech and quite "openly" as over against "secretly."

28. Tychicus—A Christian from Asia who was a companion and friend of Paul (Acts 20:4).

29. *aphtharsia*—A love that never diminishes (A. T. Robertson).

Explanatory Notes

CHAPTER 1

Ephesians 1:1-2

Paul always regarded himself as one commissioned as an ambassador (missionary) and sent forth in behalf of Jesus Christ through a special act of the will (*thelema*) of God. It was obvious that he regarded himself as God's spokesman (2 Cor. 5:18-20; Eph. 6:20). This view is in keeping with Paul's words about himself in Acts 9.

The "saints" (*hagiois*) to whom Paul addressed his letter are individuals who have come to believe in Christ as Savior and Lord and who have actively placed their trust in him, looking to him not only for forgiveness and salvation but also for wisdom, guidance, and strength. They are persons who have set their lives apart unto God to be exclusively used by him—people whose all-consuming mission is to know and to do God's will.

The words "in Ephesus," not being found in two of the oldest and most authentic manuscripts, would seem to indicate that the letter was intended as a general letter directed to all of the churches in the province of Asia.

The "grace" and "peace" of which Paul spoke come from God the Father and "equally" from our Lord Jesus Christ. For a further discussion of these words, see footnotes 5 and 6.

Ephesians 1:3-6

Every building must rest upon a foundation that is impregnable to the rains, the floods, and the winds of time

(Matt. 7:24-27). So Paul here outlined, in brief scope, the foundation of God's plan for the redemption of sinful man, a plan which has as its ultimate goal the unity of all things in Christ. The first step of this goal is accomplished by means of God's choice of us as his sons. He "picked us out" for himself.

This plan of redemption involves each person of the Trinity—God the Father, Christ the Son, and the Holy Spirit. Furthermore, in his delineation of this plan, Paul emphasized the fact that "every stage of the work of redemption and its outcome is to contribute to the glory of God in the expression of his grace" (vv. 6,12,14).[1] Although Paul did not at this point mention the Holy Spirit or the detailed concept of the Trinity that follows in verses 3-14, and although the formal distinction of the three persons is not explicit, the three here, as always, appear in purpose, function, and work as one.[2] These divine forces, though contrasting in procedures, constitute a unique expression of Deity and are always regarded as one divine person. There is no disposition on the part of the Scriptures, at this point, to analyze and harmonize any relative antagonism of thought in the presentation of these three divine persons as constituting the one Godhead.

After all, the Bible, being neither a work of philosophy nor systematic theology *per se*, merely affirms Deity's engaging in these three respects in a joint effort to redeem the whole human race. Whatever the work of the individual member of the Trinity may be, as presented in the Scriptures, it is always in accord with this ultimate purpose of God.

The spiritual blessings that come to believers in the realm of their spiritual activities are "in the realm of our heavenly relationships" and produce in believers "heavenly qualities" that contribute to God's worldwide purpose of redemption. The initiative was on the part of God, who picked us out for himself (see footnote 9) and actually made the choice to do so before the cosmic world was founded (see footnote 10).

God's aim in the choice was that the redeemed ones should be made "holy and without blemish in his sight"— that is, in accord with his standard and not the standards of the world. Only such a people, set apart and completely dedicated unto him and to his world vision of redemption, could issue unto the "praise of the glory of his grace." Of course, the basis of it all was "the good pleasure of his will," bestowed graciously upon all those who have set themselves apart as dedicated unto his holy purpose.

In verse 5, in referring to "the adoption of children by Jesus Christ to himself" (King James Version), Paul was simply saying that God designated us for sonship beforehand (literally, horizoned us off beforehand—*proorisas*). Our adoption as children of God was in keeping with the plan that lay in the purpose of God beforehand. For my discussion of the words "mystery of his will," see footnote 22; and for the words "unto administration" (*oikonomian*) translated "dispensation" in the King James Version, see footnote 23.

Ephesians 1:7-12

Here the thought turns to the role of Christ as Lamb of God who takes away the sins of the world. It is in him that we gain our redemption—our deliverance from our sins and our old life-style—whereby we become his possession; and this experience is procured for us "through his blood" because of "the riches of his grace." All who place their trust in him as Savior and Lord, whether Jew or Gentile, obtain complete emancipation and deliverance from their sins.

This emancipation (by analogy, as the setting free of a slave by his master) was accomplished by means of the blood of Christ which is referred to here as the ransom used in the process of liberation. Sinful man is set free literally at the "cost" of Christ's blood on the cross.

There is nothing, of course, to suggest that a "price" was paid to anyone. It was simply God's way of projecting himself in his Son so as to effect a plan of redemption that embraces "all things," meaning that God's redemptive effort is designed to bring about one "harmonious whole," including both Jew and Gentile (footnote 11; cf. footnotes 5,9).

The true heirs of God are the saved, whether Jew or Gentile. God selected the Jews for a special role in preparation for the advent of the Messiah in order that all men, whether Jew or Gentile, might be heirs of God according to the eternal promises. And this glorious concept of divine choice to sonship whereby all believers are "made an heritage" took place "beforehand."

Ephesians 1:13-14

Here Paul makes clear "the guaranteed relationship of believers." All the redeemed come under the sheltering umbrella of God's redeeming love in response to their faith in his Son. Speaking directly to the Gentiles, Paul said, "In whom you also, having heard the word of the truth, the gospel of your salvation, in whom also having believed (trusted) you were sealed with the Holy Spirit of the promise" (v. 13).

This "seal" found expression as new racial groups received the gospel for the first time. For instance, the Samaritan believers under Philip's ministry experienced this form of superhuman manifestation; and it was likewise seen in the case of Peter and John at the time of their prayer and laying on of hands (Acts 8:9-17). Likewise, the presence of the Holy Spirit was experienced in the home of Cornelius when Peter preached to the Romans, thus making it clear to them that they, too, through faith in Christ Jesus, were the people of God (Acts 10:11). Similar superhuman manifestations were experienced by the early missionaries as they entered new

59

territory in their witness for Christ (1 Cor. 2:4). See also Acts 19:1-7; Romans 8:16-17; 2 Corinthians 1:20-22; Ephesians 4:30.

This "sealing" or "pledge" of the Spirit is to be regarded as the beginning of God's good work in us, which "he will perfect unto the day of Jesus Christ" (Phil. 1:6). In the sealing, God makes clear by the believers' consciousness of the Spirit's presence that they are a part of God's inheritance, looking forward to the final day of redemption and the complete realization of the heavenly promises. And the sealing is but a foretaste of what is to be at the last day. It is a precious guarantee of a relationship that is eternal and that is to find its full expression in heaven (cf. footnote 28).

Ephesians 1:15-19a

Having clearly set forth God's purpose and plan for the redemption of the world and set forth the role of each person of the Trinity in the fulfillment of that plan, Paul, by means of prayer, expressed the hope that those who have been redeemed may come to have "the spirit of wisdom and revelation with complete knowledge of him," having the eyes of their hearts so enlightened that they may come to know God's hope in their calling, "the riches of the glory of his inheritance among the saints" and "the surpassing greatness of his power" toward those who have put their trust in him.

The occasion of the prayer (1:15-16) was the word that had come to Paul of the faith of the Ephesians or any of the Gentiles. Paul was always moved by the faith of believers, and for this he would ever give thanks. The prayer life of Paul was as constant as his days, and he habitually made mention of the redeemed in his prayers.

There are three special objects of knowledge (1:18-19a) for which Paul prayed on behalf of the Ephesians or other Gentiles who had come to know the Lord. It was his prayer that their understanding and insight might be comprehensive and based upon the true spirit of wisdom and revelation. For this to take place, the saints would need to have "the eyes" of their hearts "enlightened," for only by such is the soul conditioned for "all knowing" (Prov. 1:7; 9:10).

Paul's use of the perfect participle, "having been opened," indicates that the eye-opening has already taken place and still exists.

Paul did not have in mind the kind of knowledge that is merely the solid result of reasoning or research, but rather a sort of intuitive knowledge made possible by "the spirit of wisdom and revelation" which the Father of glory gives to those who completely put their trust in him by faith.

The first item of this special knowledge is "the hope of his calling" (1:18b). This hope is really twofold. The individual needs first to understand clearly that God has initiated a worldwide plan of redemption in behalf of humanity and that each member of the redeemed community has a place in that undertaking. Secondly, the individual needs to understand how he is to fit into the larger plans of God in his effort to redeem the lost world. He needs to know what use God expects to make of him in the realization of his larger hopes for humanity.

The second object of knowledge has to do with "the riches of the glory of his inheritance among the saints" (1:18c). Paul here had in mind the "wealth" that God realizes in us as saints in whom he is glorified. The same concept relating to the inheritance of God in his people is seen throughout the Old Testament (Ex. 34:9; Deut. 9:29; Ps. 28:9).

The third object of knowledge that Paul had in mind has to do with the character of God's power as it relates to his inheritance and the realization of his hope for the people of God. He wants the redeemed to become acquainted with his power and to understand it in the full measure which he demonstrated in the resurrection of Jesus from among the dead and in his exaltation.

Paul was saying that this mighty power of God is still available for expression in those who have become new creatures in Christ by means of the power of him who works in his redeemed, inspiring them both "to will and to do of his good pleasure" (Phil. 2:13).

Ephesians 1:19*b* ff.

Paul then turned to his discussion of the grounds for the unity of all things in Christ—the basis for the plan that God projected in the advent of his Son. This ground rests, in the first place, in the exaltation of Christ (19*b*-23).

God not only (1) raised his son from the dead, but he also (2) "seated *him* on his right hand in the heavens" where he would (3) continue the administration of the holy purpose which God projected in him for the redemption of the lost world. In his new relationship his rule and authority and power and lordship is above all, for all the ages; and his (4) headship "over all things" extends to the church, which is his own body. In the church one finds the fullest possible expression of Christ on earth, for the church is the recipient of all his redemptive effort. And the church (since it is the body of Christ) is to become more and more like Christ as the old life-style gives way to the new life-style in Christ; for head and body are to be regarded as a single entity in God's effort to redeem humanity.

In Christ's resurrection from the dead and in his exaltation, the redeemed find the initial basis for their understanding of the true meaning of God's purpose for Christianity as it relates to the world.

Notes

1. William Owen Carver, *The Glory of God in the Christian Calling* (Nashville: Broadman Press, 1949), p. 94. In 1979 Broadman reprinted the book in paper binding with the title *Ephesians: The Glory of God in the Christian Calling.*

CHAPTER 2

Ephesians 2:1-10

In Ephesians 1 Paul began his discussion of the grounds for the unity of all things in Christ by outlining the significance of the exaltation of Christ. He then turned to a second phase of his argument by recounting the mutual past experiences of believers.

In verses 1-10 he considered the case of both the Jew and Gentile who were once dead in trespasses and sin but who are now made alive, being created into new persons, by Christ Jesus. Here is a perfect explanation of what Paul meant in 2 Corinthians 5:17 when he said that if any person be "in Christ Jesus," he is a new *creation* (*ktisis*)—actually a new kind of creature. The word *ktisis* is an old word used, always, of divine work.

Notice how Paul began by saying, "and you" (meaning Gentiles, v. 1), and followed in verse 3 with "we likewise" (meaning the Jews). Hereby he stated unequivocally that all humanity is to be regarded as depraved by nature and therefore gives God only dead material with which to work in the creation of the new, redeemed person.

The roots of man's failure lie in his deliberate choice to live according to his carnal desires, yielding to sinful tendencies. Paul regarded unredeemed man as being spiritually dead and completely hopeless save for the revitalizing work of God's Spirit. He used the analogy of the dead Christ, whom God purposefully raised from the dead, to illustrate his ability to raise the metaphorically dead bodies of those who reach that state by means of their transgressions (*parap-*

tomasi, "falls"). These falls occurred in the life of the unbeliever because of his old life-style, which is characterized by the word *hamartiais* (sins), which represents the deliberate, voluntary disposition of the unredeemed to pursue the life of sinfulness.

Paul further contrasted (vv. 2 ff.) the moral atmosphere of the world—with its evil ruler—with the atmosphere of those who have been made alive together with Christ and raised up and caused to "sit together with him in the heavenly places in Christ Jesus."

In the former state the unbeliever conformed to the contemporary life-style of the world, all but completely uninhibited, and doing the will of the flesh and of the mind. This means that both Jew and Gentile, being sinful by nature from birth—being engaged in willful acts of disobedience—are, by nature, "children of wrath like all the rest" (Rom. 1:18 f.).

With verse 4 Paul picked up where he left off at verse 1 and declared boldly and joyfully that God himself, in his rich mercy and because of his great love, transformed the "dead" material into a person "alive" with Christ whereby the transformed soul remains in the "saved" state. The transformation took place in the past, and it still holds!

Just as the body of Christ was dead and was raised from the grave, even so the redeemed, being "dead in our trespasses," were made alive together with him. This beautiful analogy does not stop with the resurrection, for Christ "caused us to sit together *with him* in the heavenly places."

The idea here of course is not to be taken literally. It is a metaphor—a figurative expression such as that in John 6:51-52. Paul was not talking about the bodily resurrection at the last day; nor did he seem to have any reference whatever to the redeemed of God as having any part of "rule with Christ" incident to the final consummation. The purpose of **64** this glorious transformation is that the redeemed might become (and that all might see) living examples of God's grace at work in the lives of God's people. It is all a gift of God and graciously comes to the redeemed as they become new creations in Christ Jesus.

Although in the new creation the believers are re-created as individuals, they are not abandoned and left alone. The new creation has vast implications for society. The redeemed are created in Christ Jesus "for good works," prepared beforehand by God so that we might conduct our lives in accord with them (the good works). This new life-style of the believer, marked by the good works, is made possible by his re-creation and overcomes all sectional barriers and distinctions. Coming from different racial, social, and national backgrounds, this new type of humanity is rebuilt into a single community of believers who are associated in a common covenant of hope.

Ephesians 2:11-12

The last half of chapter 2 (vv. 11-22) tells about the new humanity that is created in Christ, bringing about the perfect unification of all races, whether Jew or Gentile, as God makes all "into one new man" (v. 15).

The redeemed are forever to remember this experience (the verb *remember* is present tense [linear] and indicates that they are to "keep on remembering"), especially the Gentile Christians who formerly were "without Christ" and "without hope" (v. 12). It is well to note here that the distinction in mind incident to the Gentiles who were "in the flesh, called foreskin" was that they were uncircumcised—the physical sign of the Jewish separateness as people of God—an act that was both "superficial" and "handmade" (v. 11).

Paul was not condemning all ceremonial acts as such; rather, he was pointing out that ceremonial acts should never **65** reflect inordinate pride or distinctions among the people of God.

The "promise" to which Paul referred in verse 12 has to do with the divine promise expressed in the covenant made with Abraham and the patriarchs and which, from time to time, was renewed with the people of Israel. This historical covenant that came to Abraham's descendants found its fulfillment in the advent of Jesus, the Christ.

What is more, previously the Gentiles, though being "godly" in the world (order), had failed in their quest for God. This does not mean that they were atheists in the sense of our use of the term—Paul did not say that they had denied or rejected God. The Gentiles remained in this state until the advent of the Savior in whom they were created anew.

Ephesians 2:13-18

Here Paul turned to a discussion of this new relationship that is in Christ Jesus, and he went on to say (vv. 13-16) that in this new relationship, God's peace comes to all men through Jesus Christ. These superficial distinctions that are divisive and antagonistic are all done away with in Jesus Christ (2:14-18).

It is well to note the frequent recurrence of the phrase "in Christ" (*en Christo*) found throughout the epistle. The phrase is used to indicate the vital relationship that exists between the believer and Christ—those who have been "born of the Spirit," "born again." The expression may also refer, collectively, to his people, the church—the body of Christ (see John 3:1-8).

In other words, Jesus as Savior and Lord is the Christ of the Gentiles in the same respect that he is the Messiah of the Jews and of all who would look to God by faith. And this glorious fact was accomplished "by means of the blood of Christ" (v. 13). This makes the relationship complete and enduring and available to new generations of believers.

Well might Paul say in his letter to the Romans, "Who shall separate us from the love of Christ?" (Rom. 8:35). Mere ethnic grounds can no longer form a barrier between God and the people who seek to know his redeeming love in Christ Jesus. No one is "far away" from God merely because of his ethnic origins.

Ephesians 2:14-18 is very difficult to translate because of the dissimilarity of the English and Greek idioms. There can be no mistake, however, as to the true meaning of the thought. Stark enmity on account of religious and racial background had served to fragment the personal relationships of men and to destroy the true intent of God for humanity. A wall that never should have existed had been erected, and this wall separated the Jews and Gentiles as a whole.

There are yet many superficial, artificial walls of distinction that still separate men, but these by divine intent were all abolished through Jesus Christ "by means of his flesh" (v. 15). (It appears that the words "his flesh" refer to the incarnate life of Jesus which issued in his role as Lamb of God.)

The chasm between these separate people was increased by means of "the law of the commandments" which found expression in dogmas that were mercilessly observed. But Christ by means of his atonement proposed to create all human groups into one new humanity and by doing so much, "making peace." And in this new relationship, all people have access "by one Spirit to the Father." In Christ, no one is far off any more; but all have come near, through reconciliation, by his blood.

What is more, Christ, "having slain the enmity by himself," came and preached peace to all—whether "near" or "far" away (v. 17). This is the good news of which the gospel consists. It announces the glorious fact that there is only one approach to God for all men (whether Jew or Gentile) and **67** that all have this relationship as an unceasing privilege; and all three members of the Trinity cooperate in making possible this peace and in securing us in it.

Ephesians 2:19-22

Here Paul restated the new citizenship that is in Christ Jesus. No one is a stranger or sojourner any more in Christ Jesus. Rather, all are "fellow-citizens of the saints and the household of God."

Paul's reference to the foundation of the apostles and prophets would seem to indicate that he had in mind the teachings of the apostles and the prophets which are clearly laid down as guidelines for all men in their quest for a living relationship with God. And of this foundation, of course, Christ Jesus is himself "the chief cornerstone" (v. 20).

In verses 19-20, there seems to be implied the idea of growth and development. Only in this way can the true relationship of believers, as part of the family of God, be implemented and find full expression. The phrase "every building" is merely a figure of speech obviously referring to various racial groups embracing Christianity. There were, for instance, the Greeks, the Romans, the Jews (the first), the Samaritans, and many others. These all together are to "grow into a sanctuary holy in the Lord."

There is, therefore, to be only one commonwealth in Christ Jesus, and that commonwealth is to be as an ever-growing temple—one grand architectural masterpiece of redeemed humanity made up of all the peoples of the world.

CHAPTER 3

Ephesians 3:1-9

Paul next turned, in the opening verses of chapter 3, to his own part, his mission, in this unifying redemptive activity.

In the opening verses Paul referred to himself as "the prisoner of Christ," for he was writing from prison in Rome where he awaited trial before Nero. Paul did not regard himself as a prisoner of the Roman government but rather of the Lord, in whose service he was ministering. The words "for this cause" refer to the preceding argument concerning God's elective grace. It is interesting to note how Paul appeared to begin a prayer here which he resumed in verses 14-21 in repeating the same words, "for this cause" (*tou charin*).

Grammarians have had great difficulty with this passage. Findlay (*Expositor's Bible*) calls it an extreme instance of Paul's formless style. "The sentences are not composed; they are spun in a continuous thread, an endless chain of prepositional, participial, and relative adjuncts."

Perhaps Findlay is a bit severe in his criticism of Paul's style here, for Paul was dealing with the startling discovery of a great mystery which was for him, as it broke in upon him, an all but overwhelming experience. The mystery (*to musterion*), of course, is simply the fact that the gospel of God's elective grace, now uncovered, is available to all men of every race and nation. Apparently, up to that time the mystery was completely unknown. (It is amazing to think how slow the early disciples were to grasp the meaning of Jesus' plan for their lives and for the world. For that matter, not one of them understood that Jesus would rise from the grave. His words concerning his death and resurrection seemed to fall upon idle ears.)

Paul considered himself as entrusted with the stewardship (*oikonomia*) of God's grace. This grace was given to him with the express purpose that he share it with others: "Given unto me for you," he said. It came to him by way of divine revelation, straight from the heart of God.

And what was God's purpose concerning this mystery? Certainly it was not something that was only to be shared with a select few—and that by means of a special initiation as was the case with some of the heathen religions.

The word *mystery* was a well-known word in the religious vocabularies of Paul's day. There were current religious movements in Asia Minor that had been active for over three hundred years, and these cults were referred to as "The Mystery Religions." Whatever truth the leaders professed to have was communicated to their followers by means of special initiation ceremonies.

Not so of God's great mystery which is for all the people of the world. (In v. 3 Paul had claimed the revelation "for himself," but in v. 5 he "claims it for all the other apostles and prophets of God."[1]) The words "fellow-heirs, fellow-members, and fellow-sharers" are interesting to observe. Each word, in the Greek, is compounded of the preposition "with" (*sun-*) and a word stem by which Paul emphasized the fact that in Christ's ministry to people, the Gentiles are to share equally with the Jews. Both Jew and Gentile have a joint inheritance. What God has for one, he has for both!

In verses 7-9 Paul laid bare the thoughts and intents of his own heart in relation to this unifying mission of God in Christ Jesus. He set forth his own personal function in God's plan to share with all men the mystery of God's grace. Paul thought of himself as "a minister" (*diakonos*)—that is, a "ministering attendant," ready to carry out the commands of the One who called him. Moreover, he regarded himself as the least of all the saints. (Note how Paul made his idea emphatic by using the comparative of the superlative form of the adjective "little," which literally means "more least.") In the comparison Paul doubtless thought of the days when he had been the archpersecutor of the church. Certainly in the light of it all, he felt himself to be the "least" of the apostles (1 Cor. 15:9).

In a sense, Paul regarded his special mission as twofold. First, he had been entrusted with the mission to proclaim to the Gentiles the good news concerning the incomprehensible riches of Christ. Second, he was to throw light on the character and meaning of this good news not only for the Gentiles but also for the whole world. In other words, what was once a mystery was now "God's open secret" which he would make known to all people.

Ephesians 3:10-13

Here Paul turned from the discussion of his own mission in the unifying redemptive activity of God in Christ Jesus to the mission of the church. The mission entrusted to him, as a special messenger to the Gentiles, was, in the larger sense, also entrusted to the church in her mission. He regarded himself as an instrument of the church which was, in turn, the instrument of Christ, whose divine redemptive effort embraces the whole world.

Christ is the center in which all things unite, the bond that holds all things together. Apart from Christ there is worldwide disunity, and the result of this makes for an unending conflict between man and man and man and God. The only basis for hope in overcoming this cosmic disunity is to be realized through the redemptive work of Jesus Christ as Savior and Lord. Christ is presented in the epistle as God's instrument of reconciliation, whereas the church is presented as Christ's instrument of this overall effort on the part of God to bring his peace to the world.

The use of the church as an instrument of proclamation destined to reach all the way to principalities and powers with its soul-shaking message was in accord with the eternal purpose of God which he projected in Christ Jesus. This plan of God was not an afterthought, but something that had been laid down beforehand (*prothesin ton aionon*)—literally, "the purpose or plan of the ages." (These words might well serve as a title for the whole book of Ephesians, for the book is, in essence, a revelation of God's purpose for the redemption of all the peoples of the world.)

The words translated "much-varied wisdom" of God hark back to the use of the ancient word *poikilon* in the Septuagint translation of the Old Testament to describe Joseph's coat of many colors (Gen. 37:3). Here also we have the word *sophia*, which denotes wisdom that is lofty and heavenly in character—as well as practical.

God's church, then, is the instrument through which his wisdom (Vinson in his *Word Studies* calls it the "many-tinted wisdom of God"), in all of its beautiful variety, is to be made known to men. This wisdom of God in all of its different manifestations is to be implemented and find worthy expression through the church.

In the light of Paul's words, the mission of the church may be regarded as threefold. (1) The church is to conserve the spiritual experience and relationships of the believer. Early Christians had a soul-shaking experience with Jesus. Christ's presence and sacrificial love polarized their lives and gave them a fixed pattern to live by. This is why Paul said (2 Cor. 5:17) that "if any man be in Christ, he is a new creature." The faith of early Christians was a living experience. They enjoyed a fellowship that was literally "out of this world." (2) The church is to evangelize the unreached. The early Christians went everywhere preaching the gospel, and the central message of their testimony was Jesus Christ as Savior and Lord. And the Christians gave evidence, on every side, of their awareness of the forgiveness of sin. (3) The church is to endeavor to translate into life's interpersonal relationships the glorious character of God's wisdom in all of its much-varied forms, endeavoring always to declare the full counsel of God.

Ephesians 3:14-21

Here in verse 14 the prayer that apparently was interrupted at the beginning of chapter 3 continues. One cannot be certain, of course, that Paul was beginning a prayer in verse 1, but it would seem so. Calvin thought that Paul must have knelt as he dictated this prayer. The words "every family" suggest that Paul had in mind all the various classes of people who receive the name of family from God, for God is the Father of all. He is the Father of Jesus; he is the Father to whom we have access (2:18; 3:12); he is the Father of glory, the glorious Father; he is the Father of all; he is the Father to whom all thanks must be given (5:20); he is the pattern of all true fatherhood.[2]

There are really five petitions in this great prayer of Paul (Dr. A. T. Robertson thought it was his greatest recorded prayer). Each petition is introduced by the same Greek conjunction (hina). The petitions are progressive, as Dr. W. O. Carver has pointed out, with the objective of the first petition being found in the second, and the second in the third, and so on. "They are all interlocked as the soul of the petitioner moves toward seeking the fullest satisfaction of God in his work of grace."[3] In other words, Paul was looking forward to the ultimate, grand, and final realization of all things in Christ.

In the first petition, Paul prayed that the church may become a suitable and permanent dwelling place for Christ (vv. 16-17a).[4] Christ has no dwelling place in man save in his heart—in the inner, moral, ethical self.

The follower of Christ, therefore, must be more than an ordinary man; he must have powerful resources that are beyond the merely physical element of life. This power, this strength, comes through the dynamic (*dunamei*) operation of God's spirit. He alone can make man strong. The Spirit of God alone can empower man for his divine mission as a part of the church.

Secondly, Paul prayed that the people of God who are engaged in Christ's world-redemptive mission would be able "to comprehend with all the saints what is the breadth and the length and the height and the depth" of this surpassing love and to know this love by their own experience, being thoroughly rooted and built up in it.

Every believer is to have an intimate, personal acquaintance with the divine principle which is at work in the lives of all believers through the church. By having experienced this love principle, one is able to share with others the true meaning of this cooperative, redemptive relationship of which God is the author and which he set forth in his Son.

Note how Paul summarized the riches of God's love by using the words *breadth, length, height,* and *depth.* This love embraces all people, in all the ages, and extends to every level of human need. And it is through the church, the cooperative relationship of believers, that this love of Christ is realized in its loftiest form.

Third, Paul brought his petitions to a grand climax in his prayer (19*b*) that the church may be "filled with respect to all the fullness of God."

The redeeming Christ is able to do superabundantly more than we ask or think. It is his power that works in us and brings about the miracle of transformation so that the body of believers will become, in Christ Jesus, the fitting instrument of his redemptive grace.

In the doxology that closes chapter 3, Paul, in a unique

way, emphasized the continuity of this redemptive effort of God in Christ Jesus, working through us, his body, unto whom is to be the glory. And the work of the church and its glory, though varying according to the pitiable weaknesses of people (who, though redeemed, are yet in the flesh), is to go on forever and hence "unto all the generations of all the ages" (v. 21).

No earthly power will ever be able to terminate this unifying mission of God in Christ Jesus for the redemption of all the people of the world.

Notes

1. A. T. Robertson, *Word Pictures in the New Testament* 4 (Nashville: Sunday School Board of the Southern Baptist Convention, 1931), *in loco*.
2. William Barclay, *The Letters to the Galatians and Ephesians* (Philadelphia: The Westminster Press, 1954), *in loco*.
3. William Owen Carver, *The Glory of God in the Christian Calling* (Nashville: Broadman Press, 1949), p. 136.
4. Ibid.

CHAPTER 4

Beginning with chapter 4 and continuing through chapters 5 and 6 of Ephesians, the emphasis is on the development of the new life-style of the Christian. Paul was obviously concerned that the man of faith become also a man of action. Like James, he was fully aware of the role of faith in the life of the believer; but he was also deeply concerned with the matter of works in believers' lives. He joined together, therefore, in the epistle, in a beautiful way, the concept of *inner faith and outer service*. After all, if the faith of the believer does not issue in the development of a new pattern of living that is in accord with truth, the impact of the believer's faith is likely to be negligible on the unbelieving world.

Ephesians 4:1-6

The opening verses of chapter 4 of Ephesians amount to a stirring call to unity. Paul wanted the redeemed to be diligent in their concern for the church and to do all in their power to maintain a peaceful spirit of unity.

To achieve this, the Christian must manifest a spirit of humility and meekness and patience in his relations with his fellowman. One cannot live his life apart from the interests and the welfare of the body (the church), for he is a part of that body and Christ is its head.

For one to be a meek person he must have modesty and a certain "lowliness" of spirit. Whatever self-knowledge he possesses should stem from and be based on the life-style of Christ with respect to the commands of God.

A meek man is mild and gentle in his relationships with others. He has disciplined his natural urges—the basic drives that come to him by nature—and has arrived at the point in life where his total self is completely subject to the disciplines of the Christian calling. There is hardly a more powerful adjective in the New Testament than the adjective "meekness" in verse 2.

What is more, the patience of the believer is to be unfailing; and he is to bear up his Christian brother in love. There is to be no place for irritating, discouraging attitudes in his relationships with his fellow Christians.

In verse 3 Paul went on to say that the disposition of the believer—the prevailing mood of his mind and heart—is to protect (that is, guard) the unity of the body. Paul had in mind, of course, the entire spiritual body of believers; but the same disposition is to find application in relation to the local body of believers. This togetherness is made possible by the constraining bond of "peace." Peace helps to hold the body together, thereby making it possible for the Holy Spirit to cooperate with the individuals within that body in achieving the desired unity. The situation never reaches the perfect ideal on earth, for all are in the flesh and are constantly battling with the pull of fleshly desires. But the process continues, for there is always a striving for the ideal on the part of the redeemed in cooperation with the Holy Spirit.

This hoped-for unity must rest upon a trustworthy foundation (vv. 4-6). It is interesting to note how Paul referred to the elements of this foundation. Without the use of a verb, he merely named them, one by one. Only two of the seven factual elements are qualified by so much as a word. Let us note the foundation as Paul set it forth.

1. "One body": Paul seemed to have in mind here the total body of believers who have, by the divine act of regeneration, been born of the Spirit. Every believer, of all the ages, is a part of this body. Correspondingly, the same ideal of complete oneness is to be visibly present in the local church, which is a part of the whole.

2. "One Spirit": Expositors in general seem to agree that Paul referred here to the Holy Spirit who is "the vitalizing, energizing, enlightening, and guiding spirit of the Body."[1] This interpretation is in accord with the words of Jesus (John 16:7-10) when he promised his disciples to send the Holy Spirit to abide with them and work with them in the accomplishment of his ideal for them and for the world.

3. "One hope": This word harks back to Ephesians 1:18 and means God's hope. All man-imposed limitations are to be done away with in the new hope that is in Christ Jesus. All of the redeemed are to share actively in this hope and principle.

4. "One Lord": Even as Christ became "the Lamb of God" who takes away the sins of the world, as men turn to him with repenting hearts of faith, even so he is to be Lord of all.

5. "One faith": The idea here apparently refers to the believer's experience as a Christian. Those who become sons of God put their trust in him through faith in Jesus Christ. The idea is not that of a formal, stated creed or catechism but that of the believer's experience in Christ that all Christians share and by which all are drawn together in a unifying hope.

6. "One baptism": These words refer simply to Christian baptism, the public act of commitment made by the individual in his testimony to his faith in the risen Christ and in the risen life and in his desire to identify with all others who have gone before him in the quest for the new life in Christ (Rom. 6:1-11; Col. 2:12).

The matter of modes of baptism was no question in Paul's day, for such did not arise until later. In contemporary churches, of course, there is an utter lack of oneness with reference to the meaning of and reason for baptism. But Paul obviously had in mind here only the significance that inheres in the word *baptism*, and that is the same for all believers.

7. "One God": The words "Father of all" refer not to men in general but to those who have become believers, for it is that group which Paul had in mind here. The universality of God in relation to creation and the material universe is one thing; his universal Fatherhood in relation to believers is quite another.

Ephesians 4:7-16

In these verses Paul began to deal with the individual responsibility that rests upon each member of the church. The same grace of God has been given to all, and each individual is to be aware of this heritage in Christ and to be responsible, in return, with reference to the corporate unity of the body of believers. As a member, he is to act responsibly in all matters that pertain to his interpersonal relationships with both God and man. Each believer, each member of the church, is a distinct and separate entity in the mind of Christ.

In verses 8-13 Paul dealt at some length with the diversity of the "spiritual gifts" that are likewise discussed in 1 Corinthians 12. These charismata are bestowed by the Father according to his own will, but always to the same end—namely, to glorify God, to serve man, and to bring to the believer happiness in well-doing. Paul apparently turned back to the words of Psalm 6:8, which portray God in his triumphant return from the victory over his enemies, bearing rich gifts from the kingdoms over which he triumphed.

The victory of Christ, of course, refers to his triumph of the cross as Lamb of God and his return to the Father, giving at the same time his gifts of love to men.

Paul's words "took captivity captive" (v. 8) seem to refer to the incarnation ministry of Jesus. He obviously had in mind the persons who, by faith, identified with him, and by so much were captured disciples fully recognizing his lordship and becoming, in turn, his "slaves" (*douloi*). Now they fully belong to him.

The words "lower part of the earth" seem merely to refer to the earth—location of the incarnation—the earth being regarded as lower than heaven. In other words, the same one who "came down" is the one who "ascended" so that "he might give fullness to all things" in keeping with his mission as Redeemer.

Now in order to accomplish his purpose as Redeemer, it was necessary for Christ to have special leaders to assist him in the mission. Consequently, as Paul observed here, Christ gave some the gifts (the ability) to serve in the capacity of apostles, some as prophets, some as evangelists, and some as shepherds and teachers; and all of these were to share in the effort to enlist the people of God in building up the body of Christ in the hope of achieving that oneness of faith and knowledge that leads to the mature man in Christ.

The first leaders mentioned seemed to have as their special responsibility the inauguration of the work of the church in the respective communities. Like Barnabas and Paul (and others), the apostles were missionaries in every sense of the word. The "prophets" apparently were counted upon to pick up where the apostles left off and to give guidance and direction (under the leadership of the Holy Spirit) to these newly formed Christian communities of believers. When the missionaries (apostles) and the prophets accomplished a measure of solidarity and unity in the new community of believers, they apparently moved on to other locations.

The "evangelists," in like manner, would take over where the apostles and prophets left off and would endeavor to further strengthen and expand the program begun by others until it embraced the larger community.

The "shepherds and teachers" were those who ministered in the local churches as the permanent leaders.

The overriding purpose of the efforts of all these spiritual leaders was to be the attainment of spiritual maturity having true Christian stature. In this way, the extension of Christ's kingdom would not be hindered by the kind of instability, immaturity, and gullibility that toss young Christians about as in a storm at sea, exploited by every kind of teaching and clever panderers of error.

All of this effort on the part of Christ's followers is to lead into the development of one harmonious whole in which the growth derives from Christ, the head of the body. And the growth and development are to be accomplished in the spirit of love which, in turn, produces the harmony of an inspired relationship.

Ephesians 4:17-24

Paul then turned in his argument with an impassioned plea for the abandonment of the old life-style that marked the followers of Christ prior to their regeneration. The line of separation between the Christian and the nonbeliever is to be clear and well defined. From the standpoint of ethics and morals, the believer is to live a "segregated" life. Only in this way is he able to become the new type of humanity (2:15-19) of which Paul spoke.

Paul boldly called on every follower of Christ to live like a Christian, following Christ as the perfect ideal in all ethics and morals. Believers are to have no part of the low ideals and standards of the heathen communities in which they live. Rather, they are to be "separate" in their manner of living. The depravity that marks the heathen, as outlined here by Paul, reminds one of his words in Romans 1 where there is a similar delineation of the life-style of nonbelievers.

In verses 20-24 Paul afforded us a brief glimpse of the Christian standard of living as it found expression in the life of Jesus. The followers of Jesus are to be people of humility and meekness who are literally the "slaves" (*douloi*) of Christ. Being in him, and having been incorporated into his church, they are to pass completely under the control of his mind and will, striving to have the same mind which was in Christ Jesus (Phil. 2:5 ff.). The old human self is to be disciplined completely in favor of the "new man" who is in Christ (2 Cor. 5:17). The depraved practices of the old life-style are to be abandoned forever as the believer is clothed with the "new humanity" that is in full accord with the embodiment of the mind and the will of God as seen in Christ.

Ephesians 4:25 to 5:14

Paul then began a plea for the Christian believers to live in a gracious, loyal, and loving relationship that is in keeping with the intended daily life of the people of God. Believers are to speak the truth with each other and to put away all that is false and unreal. Even in anger, there is to be no place for sin; and one is not to let the sun set on one's wrath!

In verses 26-31 Paul sketched in bold outline the natural and Christian attitudes as they stand in opposition to each other. Anger is to be restrained, suppressed, and totally overcome. There is to be no place for stealing, but rather sustained respect for the property of others. No one is to engage in corrupting speech (literally, "rotten"), for speech is the index of one's character; and when it is "rotten," it corrupts both the speaker and the one to whom he speaks.

Kindness and love are to prevail and become lifelong virtues; and Christians are to have a forgiving spirit in their relations with each other just as God in Christ does toward us (v. 32)!

Note

1. William Owen Carver, *The Glory of God in the Christian Calling* (Nashville: Broadman Press, 1949), p. 143.

CHAPTER 5

Ephesians 5:1-2

In the preceding verses (4:31-32), Paul challenged the followers of Christ to show forth in their interpersonal relationships the same kind of graciousness that God manifests toward the redeemed. God is our example, and we his children are to endeavor to become (get to be) his imitators. Jesus had said to his disciples, "I am the way" (John 14:6), and evidently Paul took his words literally. Here he said that Christ's followers are to take God as their standard. Just as he gave up his life on the cross in a substitutionary manner as Lamb of God, instead of the offerings and sacrifice which had prevailed in the Hebrew system, even so, the followers of Christ are to manifest in all their relations with one another that same spirit of self-sacrifice and gracious love.

Here one comes to the heart of Paul's concept concerning the new life-style of the believer, remembering how the self-sacrifice of Christ was pleasing and acceptable in the sight of God and bringing the redeemed into a new identifying relationship with God through Christ his Son.

Ephesians 5:3-5

The redeemed are to guard themselves meticulously against sexual immorality. This word of Paul, so desperately needed in his day, is needed no less in our own time. In Corinth especially, as well as throughout the Roman empire, sex corruption was rife both in high and in low places. The decaying paganism of the Christian era was marked by unbelief and licentiousness, with the latter issuing from the former. Paul went so far as to say that such moral debauchery should not even be mentioned in conversation (v. 3). The word Paul used for the translation "not even to be named" is *mede onomazestho* and literally means "to give not a name to." The ancient Greeks held that to talk about an evil and undesirable thing was to bring it a step nearer to favor and action.

The ancient gods of the pagan world, called by Thomas Carlyle "mud-gods," were set up in the high places of Paul's day and lent their approval to the uninhibited acts of immorality that pandered to the lusts of the flesh. Paul said bluntly **83** in verse 5 that no fornicator or impure person (or one who is covetous) will have an inheritance in Christ's kingdom.

Ephesians 5:6-7

Here Paul warned believers not to be deceived by those who would lead one astray with empty words. Because of such the wrath of God comes upon those who so respond to sexual perversion that they are actually called "sons of disobedience."

It is incredible that in Christian communities today one witnesses the sort of attitude that prevails toward the so-called "gay" community and others who flaunt, openly, the age-long concepts of human sexuality observed throughout the centuries by the Judeo-Christian heritage.

Ephesians 5:8-14

Those who have passed from darkness to light are to remember that they now *are* light "in the Lord" and that as such they are to continue so to live. The Christian community is, by God's intent, a new kind of society: a new way of thinking, feeling, and acting. Such is the essence of repentance and faith for which Jesus called in Mark 1:14-15. A city that is set on a hill, said Jesus, "cannot be hid"; and his followers are to live so that the unbelieving world may observe their good works.

It is not easy for a believer to pass from the old life-style over into the new life-style of the redeemed; but such is an absolute necessity. The redeemed must abandon the mood and sinful tendencies that by nature mark the conduct of the unbelievers. Reminding Christians that they were formerly "darkness, but now . . . light in the Lord," Paul enjoined them to continue to live in this state, knowing that light only bears fruit in goodness and righteousness and truth—and all the while testing to see if the thing at hand is pleasing to God.

Paul in his use of the word *dokimazontes* (translated "testing") uncovered what may prove to be the fatal weakness in human society—a weakness that is perhaps more prevalent today than it has been in any generation—namely, the gradual loss of the ability to distinguish between the things that differ.

The redeemed are called upon to remember that they are, in their relation to Christ, the light of the world (Matt. 5:14-16). In the day-by-day human expression of that light, therefore, they are to part company with all the unfruitful works of the darkness and also to "reprove" (convict by turning the light on it) such conduct. Some of these social sins, Paul said, are done "in secret" and are too shameful for speech (v. 12).

In his use of "fruit-bearing" and "light," Paul emphasized the fact, as Dr. Carver noted, that the life of the Christian produces "conduct that is characterized by three basic attitudes and principles in human relations," namely, goodness, righteousness, and truth.[1] Note the symmetry of Paul's thought: (1) "Goodness" marks the character of the person; (2) "righteousness" marks the practical side of the disposition of the believer; (3) "truth" marks the harmonious relationship of the mind and will of God in all of the interpersonal relations of believers. This light makes everything distinctly seen and distinguishes the Christian from the person whose life is marked by the darkness of unbelief.

The Christian, therefore, is to be a discriminating person. He is to examine all things by the light of Christian truth and to act accordingly.

Paul closed his appeal (v. 14) with what may be a portion of an early Christian hymn known in his day, saying, "Wake up, you sleeper, and rise up from among the dead, and Christ will shine upon you." In Christ, one literally becomes a "new creature," experiencing a spiritual resurrection that enables him to become as a spiritual light in the midst of a **85** crooked and perverted generation (Phil. 2:15).

Ephesians 5:15-21

The community of believers is to be marked by living that is consistent with a fixed principle laid down for believers in the Word.

1. Christians are to be extremely careful (keep a sharp lookout) about how they walk around in the midst of unbelievers. They are to live ordered lives and not walk about as those who are short of wisdom.

The Christian is to be discreet in social judgment and guided by the Holy Spirit. Paul used the figure of the marketplace and admonished all believers to make the use of their opportunity (buying up your opportunity); and because "the days are evil," no time should be lost! The Christian is to be marked by rational discernment in which he constantly strives to understand the will of the Lord in relation to every human situation.

2. Paul acknowledged man's need for help in the extenuating circumstances of life such as grief, disappointment, and failure; but he reminded believers that the help comes not from beverage alcohol which issues in a state of utter hopelessness. Rather, the believer in such times of distress is to be constantly filled with the Spirit. God is always ready to afford the believer a fresh infilling of his gracious presence when the need requires it and when the believer endeavors, to the best of his ability, to live in the environment of God's control.

In these unusual experiences of life, believers are to find joy and satisfaction not through harmful excesses but rather by the fellowship of communication with one another and with God. They are to make use of music in their fellowship with one another and to always manifest a true spirit of thanksgiving (vv. 19-20).

3. In this mood of dependence upon the Holy Spirit and in the desire to implement the will of God in the total sphere of human relations, the redeemed are to subordinate themselves to one another in the fear of Christ. The whole approach, of course, is voluntary and full of ethical meaning both for the one who subjects himself and for those with whom he is involved. Here one comes to the only viable basis for collective living; for by such, the autonomy of the individual is divinely preserved. Otherwise, human personality would be stunted, warped, and without responsibility.

Ephesians 5:22 to 6:9

Paul went on to discuss this principle of subordination in relation to the family household and to apply the principle in three respects.

1. First he discussed the Christian relationship that is to prevail between the husband and wife (vv. 22-23). Obviously referring back to the mood of verse 21, Paul apparently did not see fit to use the words "subordinating yourselves" again, as some of the responsible manuscripts suggest, but went on with the idea that the wife is to subject herself in everything to her husband "as to the Lord," in the same manner in which the church is subject to the Christ (v. 24). Naturally, the wife is completely autonomous in the practice of the matter, for the initiative is to be hers.

In the Christian economy there can be no male and female but only oneness "in Christ Jesus" (Gal. 3:28). After all, the husband and wife are "joint heirs of the grace of life" (1 Pet. 3:7, RSV).

In the Christian economy a woman, for the first time, was looked upon as a person and not as a thing. Up to that time she had no legal rights. She was virtually her husband's possession. He could do with her almost as he willed.

In reality, however, there seemed to be a rather high **87** viewpoint concerning the marriage bond among the ancient Jews, for there was a saying of the rabbis, "Every Jew must surrender his life rather than commit idolatry, murder, or adultery."

In Deuteronomy 24:1 there is a summary of the law concerning divorce. If a man desired to get rid of his wife, he could give her a bill of divorcement written by a rabbi to his wife in the presence of two witnesses; and that made the divorce complete.

In Paul's day Roman family life had sunk to its worst. Women, according to Seneca, dated the years by the names of their husbands. Jerome said there was a woman in Rome who was married the twenty-third time and she was her husband's twenty-first wife.

Against this background Paul presented the Christian ideal of the husband-wife relationship.

According to God's plan, the husband is to "keep on" loving his wife in the same manner in which Christ loved the church and gave himself for her. Christ's devotion to the church is to be the example of the husband's devotion to his wife. In reality, the husband (being human) can never have the same creative relationship to his wife as Christ had to the church. Still the wife, in her spirit of subordination, is to endeavor to relate herself to her husband as Christ does to the church.

Actually, the ideal for husbands (vv. 25-31) does not differ essentially from the ideal for the wife, though it is interesting to note that Paul did not use the "high" word for love (*agape*) with reference to the wife's relationship to the husband, as he used it of the husband in his relationship to the wife. The husband is to endeavor to manifest the same quality, the same kind of unselfish love, toward his wife that Christ exercised toward the church. The unusual figure in verse 26 **88** has caused expositors considerable difficulty. What Paul appeared to have in mind is the idea of purification. The expression "in a word" seems to convey the idea of "as the saying is."

Moreover, the husband is obligated to love his wife as his own body (v. 28); for a person never hates his own flesh but rather "nourishes and cherishes it," just as also Christ did the church.

In verse 31 Paul enjoined the Christian husband to "leave" his father and mother in the sense of the former relationships and to be joined to his wife so that they may eventually become one unit, "one flesh."

In verse 32 Paul acknowledged the implied difficulty of living up to this lofty ideal in the relationship of husband and wife; but both are personally to endeavor to address themselves faithfully to the claims of God in their marriage bond.

In closing the entreaty (v. 33), Paul seemed to place the heavier responsibility upon the husband, using the imperative. In the case of the wife the imperative is not used; rather, a subjunctive, purpose clause is the means of expression.

Note

1. William Owen Carver, *The Glory of God in the Christian Calling* (Nashville: Broadman Press, 1949), p. 162.

CHAPTER 6

Ephesians 6:1-4

2.　Having discussed the relation of husbands and wives, Paul logically followed with a discussion of the relation of parents and children. Addressing the children, he followed with the imperative form of an old word *hupakouete*, which means "to hear as under another"—hence "hear and obey." The will of a child is to give way to the superior will of the father and mother. The will of a child is not autonomous as is that of the parents; for it is the responsibility of the parents to determine what is right, while the child makes the determination to do what the parents decide is best. By responsible obedience to their parents during the learning stages in which they voluntarily cooperate, children will eventually develop into autonomous self-control. Paul supported his admonition by quoting the commandment in Exodus 20:12, which gives primary significance to the commandment and also follows it with a promise of good, long life on earth.

The responsibility on the part of parents also is obvious. Their goal should be to develop in the mind of the child ethical judgment and a desire for moral living. They are not to irritate their children by using methods that are wrong. They should ever strive to nurture and guide their children in the development of a personality that is in accord with the ideal the Lord has in mind for them. The words "of the Lord" (v. 4) simply put the whole relationship of the parent to the child in matters of education and development on such a high plane that all of it relates to the Lord. This calls for great discipline on the part of parents as well as children.

Ephesians 6:5-9

3. Here Paul dealt boldly with a problem that was rife throughout the Roman empire—the problem of slavery. His words did not sanction the system of slavery; there is nothing to indicate that Christianity is back of the system. Rather, Paul hereby laid down principles that will help to do away with slavery—not through violent revolution, but rather through social and ethical determinations brought about by the expulsive power of divine ideals.

It is not an easy position that Paul called for the slaves to take, for he enjoined them to be obedient to their human masters with "fear and trembling" and with singleness of mind as to Christ. Their service is not to be performed with a view to gaining human approval but as slaves of Christ doing the will of God from the soul, and with a spirit of goodwill as slaving for the Lord and not for men. The slave is, in the meantime, to be conscious of the fact that he will receive back from the Lord whatever good things he does—whether enslaved or free. In a word, the slave is to look beyond the earthly master to the divine Maker who is his real master. And the slave is to remember that wherever he works, and whatever the human circumstance may be, as a believer he is working for the Lord.

The principle that applies to the slave applies also to the master (v. 9*a*) whose responsibility is even greater because of his position in relation to those who serve him. There are to be no threats on the part of masters in dealing with the slaves, but rather a spirit of friendliness and brotherly love. The master is to show the same Christian consideration toward the slave that he (Paul) has admonished the slave to show toward the master. After all, both the slave and the master are subject to a common Master who is in heaven and with whom there is no favoritism or respect of persons.

The Christian principles that Paul so clearly enunciated here extend to all men who serve in the master-and-workman relationship and, if applied sympathetically and intelligently, would ultimately lead to a satisfactory solution of every problem that men face in today's world in the realm of labor and management, business and economics. Surely there can be no vital society in any area of the world of men apart from the struggle for the realization of the ideals of the true Christian household.

Ephesians 6:10-20

Having set forth Christ as God's instrument and the church as the instrument of Christ in the ultimate achievement of God's purpose of redemption, and having made clear that it is the responsibility of the church to bring all men into a saved relationship with the heavenly Father, Paul then turned to the Christian's warfare—his victorious encounter with the forces of evil.

Paul was keen in his use of the vocabularies of athletes and warriors. He understood the enemies of Christ and their desire to overthrow the purpose and ethics of the Christian warrior. A learned man, he was thoroughly aware of the political, social, and economic movements of his day. Warning his fellow-pilgrims of the danger throughout his writings, he offered counsel to those engaged in the conflict.

In this spiritual war, the soldier is to find his strength "in the Lord and with the power of his might" (v. 10). The soldier is to be prepared with the same spiritual strength with which God prepared Joshua for his mission upon the death of Moses (Josh. 1:1-9). One might also think here of the words of Jesus in John 16 as he sought to prepare the twelve for their continuing mission.

The Christian warrior needs the complete armor of God, so that he may be able to stand up against the devil's crafty methods (v. 11). In contemporary society (and altogether too much so in the contemporary church), many people have seemed to lose sight of the fierce character of this warfare and of the devil who is the directing leader of the forces that oppose the Christian churches. The devil is methodical, and his plans are full of tricks and strategies. This is why the Christian needs all of God's armor if he is to be able to "stand" victoriously when the conflict is over.

This conflict is a "face-to-face" affair. Notice, in verse 12,

Paul's repeated use of the preposition "against": The wrestling, he said, is "not against blood and flesh" (i.e., man to man) but "*against* the principalities, *against* the authorities, *against* the world tyrants of this darkness, *against* the spiritual elements of wickedness in the heavenly places." Man's chief enemies are not human but demonic. These demonic personalities are arrayed on the side of the human opponents of the Christian and serve to inspire and motivate the warfare against the body of Christ.

In his use of the words "the heavenly," Paul was trying not so much to define the location of the conflict as the conflict's nature and the type of opposition the Christian faces—an opposition that arrogantly arrays itself against all heavenly concerns.

The fact that Paul used the definite article "the" with reference to "principalities," "authorities," "world tyrants," and "spiritual elements" indicates the reality of the kinds of spiritual forces that confront the Christian. He referred to them as living personalities.

We may do away with the devil in our philosophical and theological reasoning, but we cannot banish the reality of his presence and influence in our lives and, at times, in our churches.

The Christian is to "take up," therefore, God's complete armor, for by such he will be able to stand in the evil day. No part of the armor is to be left off. The words "evil day" may have reference to some special effort on the part of the unbelieving world to completely do away with the Christian movement. This is apparently Paul's warning in Acts 20:28-31; 2 Thessalonians 2:1-12; 1 Timothy 4:1-5. Perhaps a better way is to regard his words as applying to any and all conflicts where there is spiritual warfare. The important thing is for the Christian to be completely armed for the occasion. He is to be equipped and ready.

1.   "Take your stand therefore having girded your loins with truth" (v. 14). Just as the soldier's belt gives a feeling of strength to the body, so will the inner consciousness of one's own integrity, in the sight of God, enable him for the conflict. The Christian is therefore to gird his loins "with truth." He is to be a man who is completely devoted to and undivided in his loyalties to the teachings of God's Word.

2.   "And having put on the breastplate of righteousness" (v. 14). Just as the breastplate of the warring soldier of Paul's day served to protect the vital parts of his body, even so righteousness on the part of the Christian soldier is essential to his protection. This righteousness of God is by faith, and it is both "imputed" and "imparted" (see Rom. 1:17; 3:30). "My strength is as the strength of ten," said Tennyson, "because my heart is pure."

3.   "And having shod your feet with the readiness of the gospel of peace." The soldier is to be ready at all times to go to any and all places to share the gospel of peace which God makes available to all in the blood of the Christ. Having the peace of God first in his own heart, the fighting soldier of God is to be ready to go out upon rescue missions in the effort to redeem all others from sin unto salvation.

4.   "In everything taking up the shield of the faith" (v. 16). The Roman soldier had a shield that was large enough to protect his whole body. With this he could effectively stop any of the darts (though pitch-dipped and set on fire) that the enemy might hurl against him. Christian faith is invincible!

5.   "And receive the helmet of salvation." Note how Paul passed from the use of the participle here to that of the imperative form of the verb just as he did in verse 13. In verse 13 he said "take up," but here he used the simpler form "take" with the meaning "receive." The helmet is the consciousness of salvation. The man who has passed (spiritually) from death unto life knows that he need have no fear of

mortal man, for mortal man can never lay hands on his soul.

6. "And the sword of the Spirit." This sword is simply the Word of God. The author of Hebrews 4:12-13 describes the character of this sword, the Word, in a striking manner. Isaiah (11:4; 49:2) used it as a weapon of the Messiah. In Revelation, chapter 1, John used a similar figure. The Christian warrior is to use this sword because it is God's will for him to do so and because it is the believer's chief weapon in dealing face to face with the adversary.

Last of all, the Christian warrior is to be a man of "prayer and supplication" (v. 18). This mood of prayerful watchfulness is to prevail on every occasion and is always to include an entreaty for all the saints (v. 18). No mention is made of specific objects of prayer, but the assumption is that the objective is to be victory in every phase of the encounter.

Paul also asked for prayer in his own behalf, as Christ's ambassador in a chain (vv. 19-20). This call for prayer, on Paul's part, is characteristic of his petitions on other occasions. (See Rom. 15:30-32; 2 Cor. 1:10-11; Phil. 1:19; 1 Thess. 5:25; 2 Thess. 3:1-2.) Here in his petition for prayerful support as an ambassador of Christ, Paul mentioned three phases of his objective: (a) that he might have the right message and readiness of speech; (b) that he might not be bound down by circumstances of his imprisonment but that he might speak "boldly" in sharing the message God gave to him for the world; (c) that he might faithfully discharge his responsibility in making known the "mystery" of the gospel (v. 19b). Paul wanted to be sure that he was courageous, unto the uttermost, in all matters that had to do with his proclamation of the gospel. After all, this was the core of his calling as an ambassador of Christ.

Ephesians 6:21-24

Paul closed his message with some final words that pro- **95** vide information concerning himself (vv. 21-22) and followed with a word of peace and love to all of his brothers in Christ Jesus. He wanted his friends to understand his present situation and spoke of Tychicus, the bearer of the letter and a chief helper. Tychicus was one of those who accompanied Paul with the relief funds to Jerusalem (Acts 20:3 ff.). He was obviously one in whom Paul had great confidence, and it is quite likely that he shared the Ephesians letter with all the churches of Asia.

In the closing words of benediction (vv. 23-24), Paul manifested his concern that "peace" and "love" and "faith" and "grace" continue to be with all who are constant in their love for our Lord Jesus Christ—and untainted with corruption.